Chelsea!
The Ultimate
Fan Book

Pete Collins

B⬛XTREE

PETE COLLINS is a freelance writer who regularly contributes to Chelsea's matchday magazine and club newspaper *Onside*. He is a season ticket holder and a child at heart.

Edited by Neil Barnett, editor of Chelsea's *Matchday Magazine* and club newspaper *Onside*. He has also edited or written *The Chelsea Quiz Book*, *The Chelsea Fact File* and *Blue Heaven – The Full Story of Chelsea's Historic 1997-98 Season*, all published by Boxtree.

First published in the UK in 1998 by Boxtree,
an imprint of Macmillan Publishers Ltd, 25 Eccleston Place, London SW1 W 9NF and Basingstoke

Associated companies throughout the world

Further material supplied by Gill Lester
Illustrations by Rob Anderson

All photographs supplied by Action Images except: page 14 – Steev Burgess and pages 64, 82, 83, 85, 86, 87 - Neil Barnett

ISBN: 0 7522 2468 9

10 9 8 7 6 5 4 3 2 1

Design by DW Design

Printed and bound in Great Britain by The Bath Press

A CIP catalogue entry for this book is available
from the British Library

ACKNOWLEDGEMENTS

The contributors would also like to thank Carina Bell and Kate Booth for their help with the book.

CONTENTS

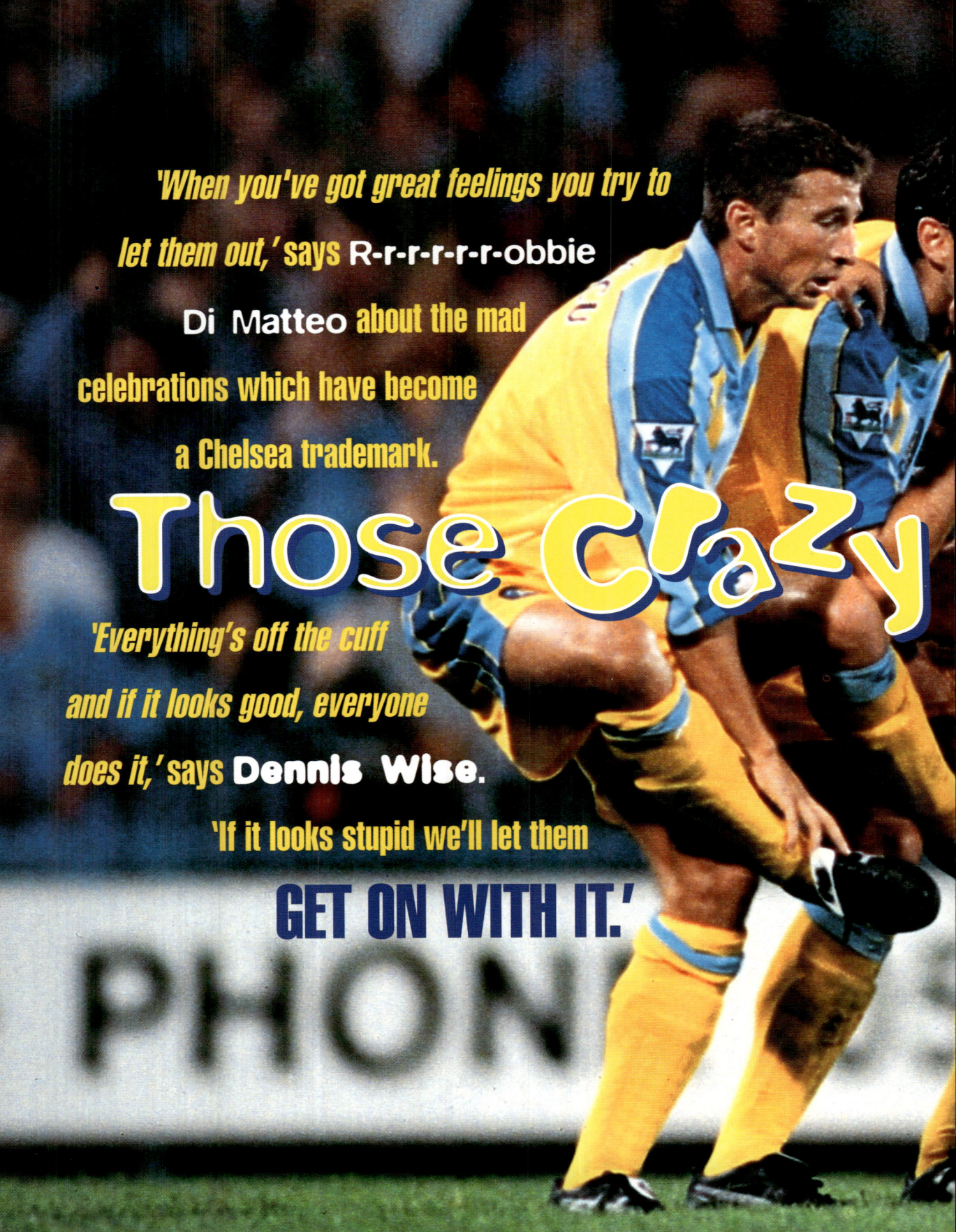

'When you've got great feelings you try to let them out,' says R-r-r-r-r-obbie Di Matteo about the mad celebrations which have become a Chelsea trademark.

Those Crazy

'Everything's off the cuff and if it looks good, everyone does it,' says **Dennis Wise**.

'If it looks stupid we'll let them

GET ON WITH IT.'

Celebrations

Here are our favourite goal celebrations – **what are yours?**

1 **Roberto Di Matteo's trip around Wembley, 43 seconds into the 1997 Cup Final** – because we'd waited so long.

2 **The Statue, after Robbie Di Matteo's goal against Middlesbrough, August 1996** – because 'everyone seems to like that one', says Dennis Wise.

3 **The Slaphead: Wisey again, October 1995** – 'Up at Aston Villa a bald-headed fella had been giving me stick all the way through the warm-up; so when I scored I slapped me head. He knew who he was.'

4 **Cleaning Dan Petrescu's boots after his first goal at home to Tromsø in the Cup Winners' Cup, November 1997** – 'When we realised he'd scored with his head, we just started cleaning his boots,' says Robbie Di Matteo.

A celebration is born - vs Middlesbrough, 1996

Wisey slaps his head - vs Aston Villa, 1995

celebr

5 **The Chair, after Robbie's goal at Crystal Palace, September 1997** – 'Sometimes you sit on a chair like this,' says Robbie.

6 **Wisey's T-shirt message to Gianluca Vialli, vs Derby, January 1997** – because it all worked perfectly.

7 **Zola's Knees-Up in the FA Cup semi-final vs Wimbledon, April 1997** – great goal, great celebration.

8 **Worshipping Paul Hughes after his debut goal against Derby, January 1997 –**
'That was nothing to do with me. The boys just turned it into a great celebration, going down on their knees. It was brilliant,' says Hughes junior.

'When I scored in the Cup Final, I was just going crazy. I don't know where I was running to. If my team-mates hadn't stopped me I'd still be running.' Roberto Di Matteo

9 **The Granny Granville silly walk after scoring a late goal at home to Slovan Bratislava, September 1997 –** 'He got a little bit excited, like Graeme Le Saux,' says Wisey.

10 **The Once Every Sixty Years as Wisey got sucked five rows into the Chelsea away support following his winning goal at Anfield, February 1992 –** Well, t doesn't happen often.

Wisey invites Luca to cheer up, 1997

'It was a time when Luca was going through a bad patch. I just did it to cheer him up. It was the first time I ever wrote anything on a T-shirt and I scored straight away. Maybe I should do it more often.'

Wisey on his T-shirt message to Luca Vialli

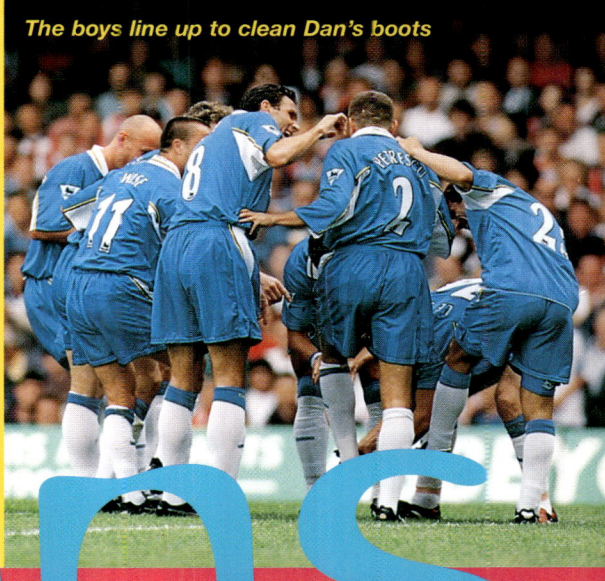
The boys line up to clean Dan's boots

THE WORST CELEBRATION

Graeme Le Saux's first goal on returning to Chelsea against Palace when he ran and jumped across the pitch like a motorised windmill.

'He got a little bit carried away and we got a bit embarrassed for him. We let him get on with it because he looked rather stupid. He was like a little kid who'd just scored his first goal.' Dennis Wise

7

Best meal: 'Pie and mash.'

Worst meal: 'Anything with garlic, it makes your breath stink. And anything that Sian and Lisa cook at the training ground.'

Best CD: 'Tony Ritchie Project.'

Best computer game: 'I always liked the old Space Invaders. I thought it was brilliant.'

Best goal: 'Mine against Viktoria Zizkov, a 30-yarder, left foot, top corner.'

Wisey. The Rat. Home fans love him, the opposition's fans hate him – the mark of a feared practitioner. Captain and Chelsea legend, Dennis has added skill and vision to his incredible will to win during his time at Chelsea. He came from Wimbledon in 1990, a Cup winner and with a reputation as a winger, but has developed into a fine midfielder, whether in the 'holding' role or with more licence to roam. He's been a Cup-winning captain three times but you can sense he wants more...

WISEY UNPLUGGED

Best subject at school: 'I don't know, I didn't go that much! But I did like PE.'

Nickname at school: 'It's always been Wisey, but I'm also known as The Rat at the club.'

Do you still support the team you did when you were young? 'I used to support QPR because my dad's friend played for them. I don't really support them any more.'

Does being short have its advantages? 'Sometimes it has when you get in trouble on the field with the referee. If you're short and you smile, you'll get away with it.'

If you were a pop star, who would it be? 'Elvis Presley. I used to love his records. I was really surprised when I found out Gazza did too. When we were training for England together, we both started to sing along to the songs in his car.'

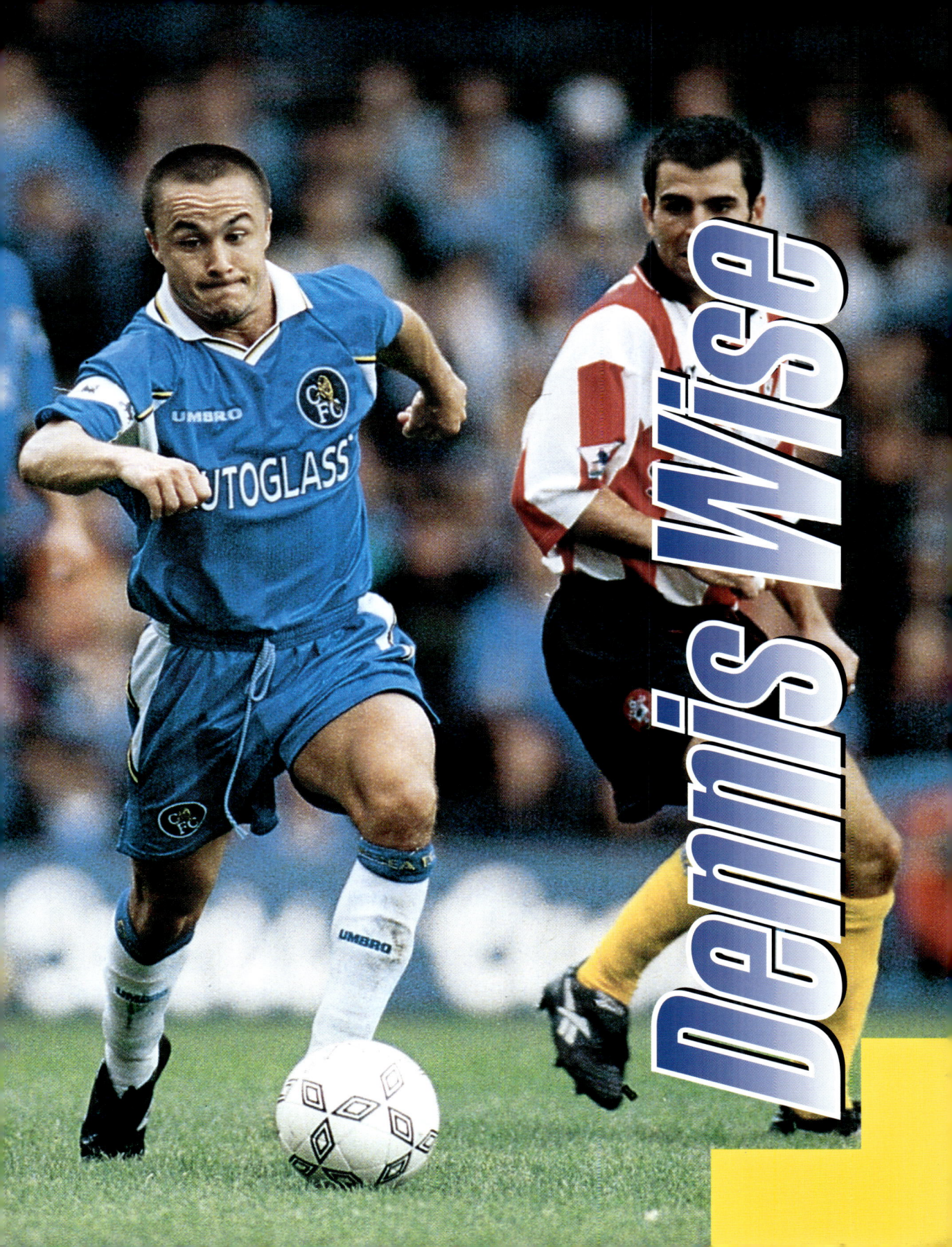

Dennis Wise

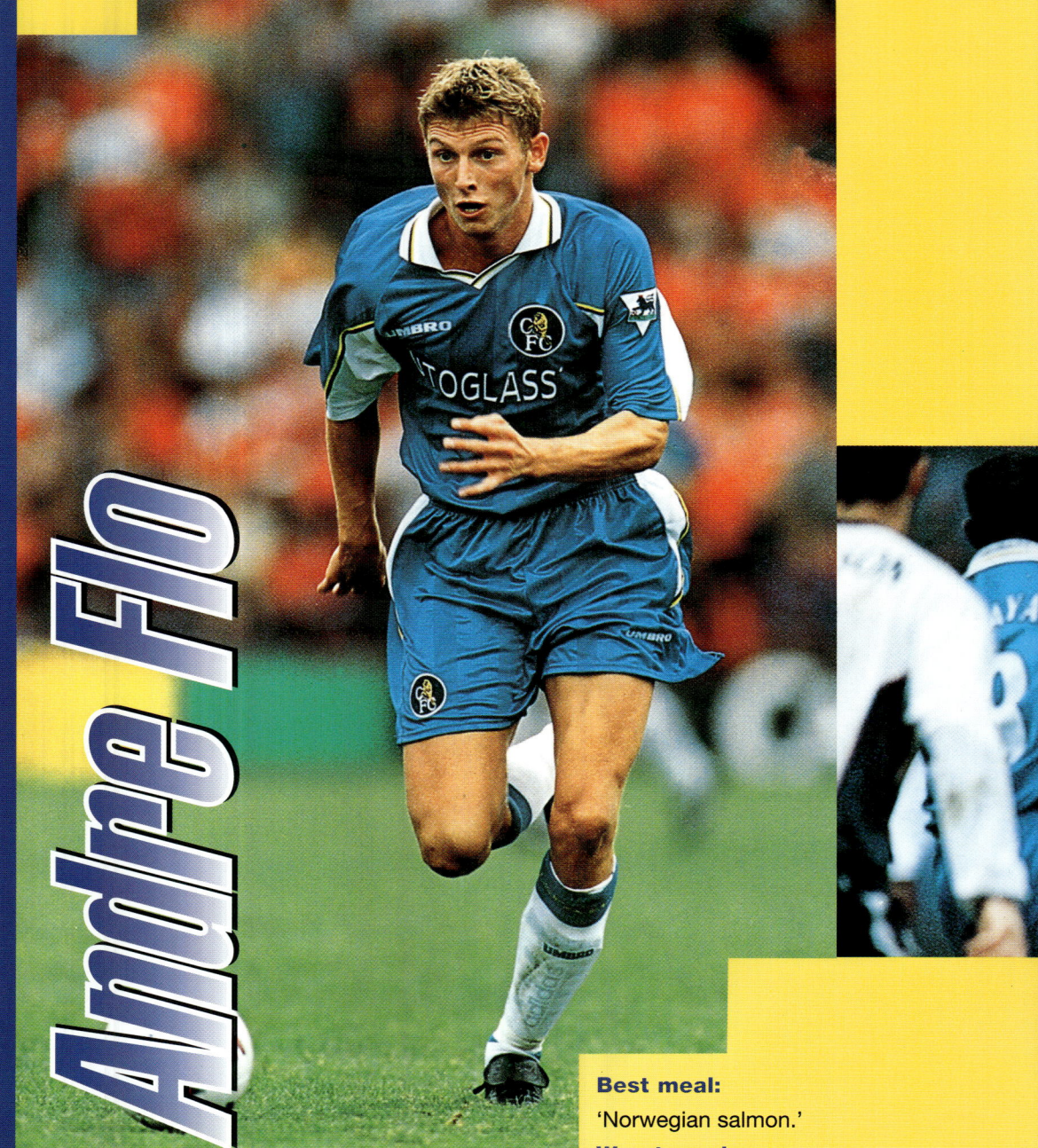

Tore Andre Flo

Best meal:

'Norwegian salmon.'

Worst meal:

'Kebab.'

Best CD:

'Celine Dion.'

Best computer game:

'I think the car games, the racing.'

Best goal:

'My second against Betis away maybe. It felt so very good.'

Best meal:
'Steak and chips.'
Worst meal:
'Anything with Brussels sprouts.'
Best CD:
'Usher.'
Best computer game:
'Fifa '98.'
Best goal:
'Roberto Carlos' free-kick against France for Brazil in Le Tournoi is the best goal I've ever seen.'

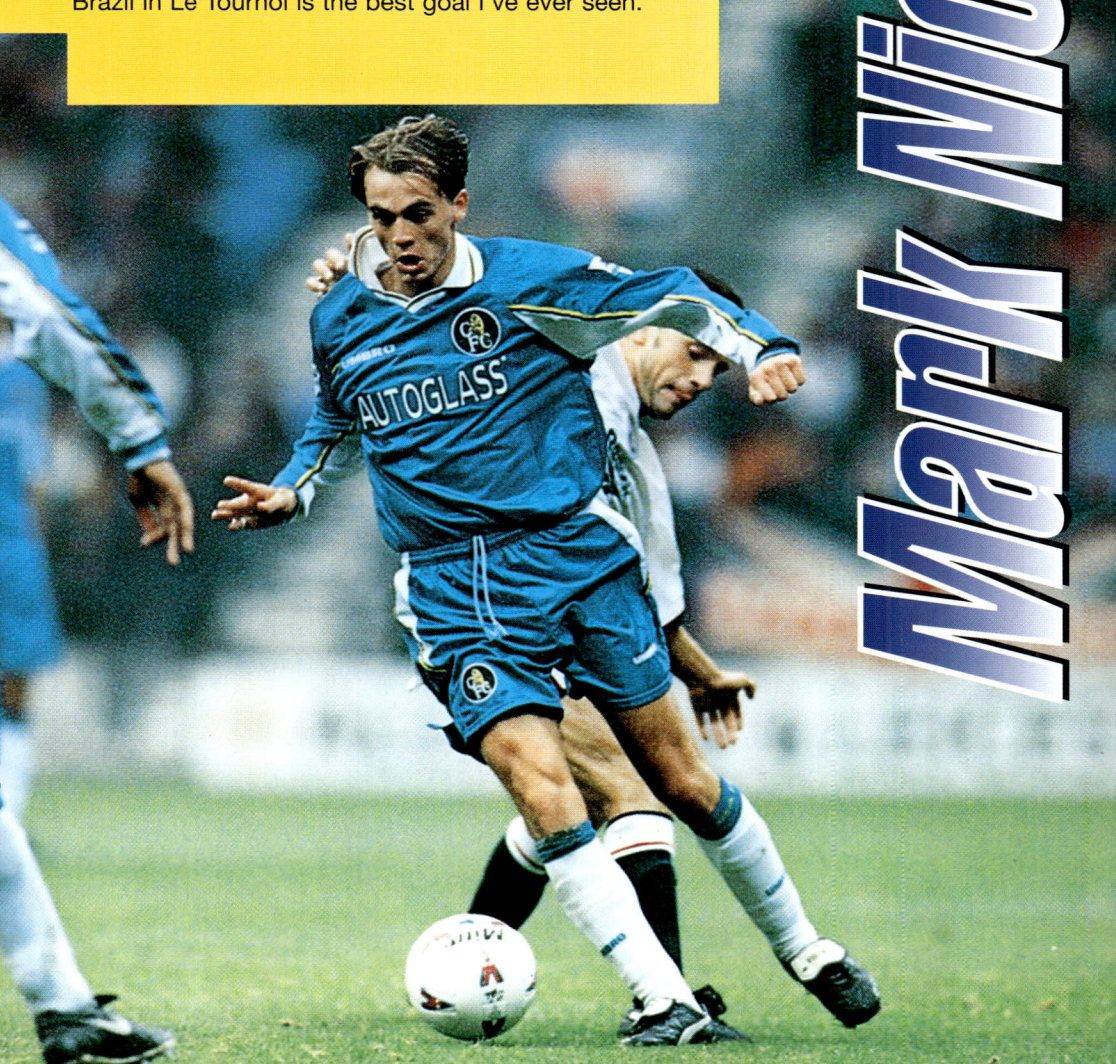

Mark Nicholls

BLUE BOY

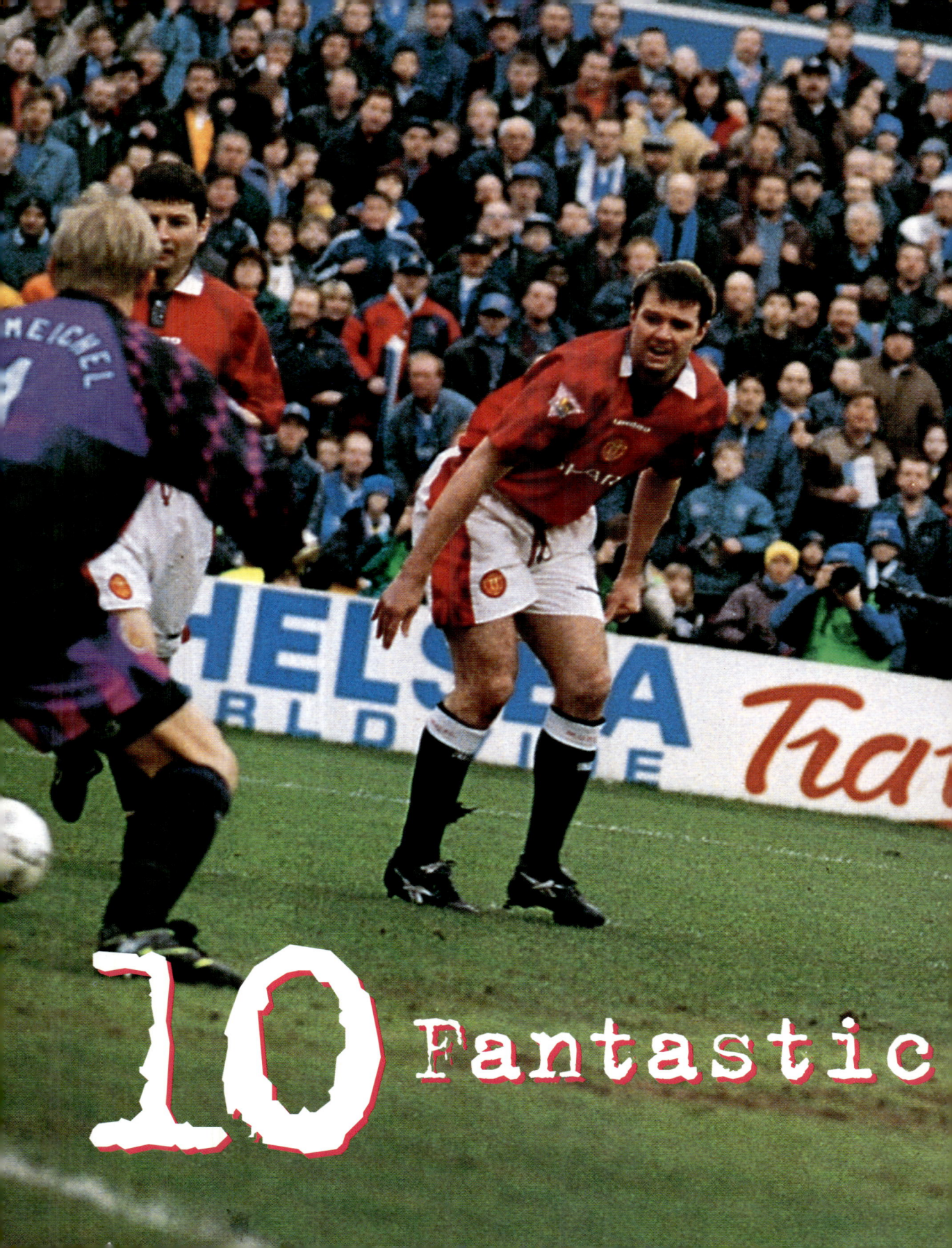

10 Fantastic

Chelsea Goals

Franco beats Peter Schmeichel, February 1997

1 **Gianfranco Zola against Wimbledon,**
FA Cup semi-final at Highbury, 13 April 1997
Franco takes the defender with him as he runs right to left across the edge of the penalty area to receive Di Matteo's pass, then he back-heels the ball to himself, wrong-footing the defender, turns swiftly and shoots low into the right-hand corner, sending the Chelsea gathering mad.

2 **Robbie Di Matteo against Middlesbrough**
FA Cup Final at Wembley, 17 May 1997
Just 43 seconds in, Robbie gets the ball

4 **Gianfranco Zola against Derby County,**
Premiership, 29 November 1997
Franco back-heels to Di Matteo, turns to receive the instant return, gets clear and shoots past Poom from an angle to record his first hat-trick. 'The action was perfect. Robbie's pass was magnificent. The game must be sent to schools,' says Franco.

5 **Frank Leboeuf against Leicester City,**
Premiership, 18 October 1997
With time running out at 0–0 and Chelsea pushing forward, Frank takes Vialli's pass in

Chart-topper – Franco's semi-final goal against Wimbledon

from Wisey, moves into the Boro half at pace, with Hughesy taking the defender away, and unleashes a thunderbolt. From then on there was little doubt that Wise *would* go up to lift the FA Cup.

3 **Gianfranco Zola against West Ham,**
Premiership, 21 December 1996
Franco takes Hughesy's pass, turns hard-man Dicks inside out on the edge of the area, not once but twice, and shoots past Miklosko.

midfield and sends an unstoppable rocket into the top right corner. Stamford Bridge erupts. 'For me it is the most beautiful shoot I ever do,' Frank says.

6 **Dan Petrescu against Southampton,**
Premiership, 30 August 1997
Taking the ball in midfield, Dan runs away from a challenge and from 20 yards chips the ball perfectly over 'keeper Jones into the far left corner. 'A great chip by Dan – magnificent goal,' chips in Wisey.

7 **Graeme Le Saux against Crystal Palace,**
Premiership, 13 September 1997
With Chelsea cruising at 2–0, Soxy surges past a hesitant defence and crashes a rising shot in off the post from 16 yards. 'My first goal for Chelsea was in that same goal at Selhurst, also in the last minute,' recalls Graeme.

8 **Gianluca Vialli against Barnsley,**
Premiership, 24 August 1997
De Goey catches a corner, throws out to Petrescu on the halfway line and he sends a

inside Irwin, running across Pallister and touching the ball between Schmeichel and the near post. 'He was clever enough to go wide and caused us a lot of problems – it was a good performance from Zola,' says United manager Alex Ferguson.

10 **Ruud Gullit against Manchester City,**
Premiership, 12 March 1996
Receiving the ball in the centre circle, Ruud goes to move right, accelerates left, turns back inside and runs square, suddenly letting fly from 25 yards, scoring with

Ruud celebrates his goal against Man. City, March 1996...

... and this is how he did it

superb ball forward to the sprinting Vialli on the edge of Barnsley's area. Luca rockets an unbelievable half-volley past Watson for Chelsea's third of six. 'Now it's difficult to play in Chelsea because there are four strikers, so when you get the chance you have to score,' says Luca.

9 **Gianfranco Zola against Manchester United,** *Premiership, 22 February 1997*
A six-pass move which ends with Franco running on to a pass from Petrescu, turning

'keeper Immel rooted to the spot. 'There's not many players who can hold on to the ball for 20 seconds – that doesn't sound long, but in a game of football I can assure you it is. It was a wonderful shot,' purrs manager Glenn Hoddle.

Best meal: 'Chinese.'

Worst meal: 'Bad Chinese.'

Best CD: 'Radiohead, any one of theirs.'

Best computer game: 'Lara Croft, Tomb Raider, both I and II.'

Best goal: 'Liam Brady cut inside the penalty area and hit the top left-hand corner for West Ham. That's the first one that comes into my head.'

Back for his second spell at the club which brought him into top-class football, the England wing-back was involved in one of the strangest Chelsea transfer deals ever when he went to Blackburn with Steve Livingstone (plus £450,000) coming the other way. Graeme, known as 'Bergerac' after the Channel Island detective, went on to win a Championship medal and 20 England caps, Livingstone made one appearance for the Blues – and when Chelsea bought Graeme back, he cost a club record £5 million. Good business for Blackburn! But now he's back where he belongs and he's a Cup winner.

'BERGE' UNPLUGGED

Greatest moment in career:

'Winning my first England cap. It's the highlight of your career as a player to represent your country.'

Ambitions:

'To win a championship with Chelsea.'

Why did you become a footballer?

'I always enjoyed playing football. From an early age I wanted to be a footballer after seeing it on television.'

Memory you would erase:

'Breaking my ankle. It was a serious injury – it lives with you a long time.'

How do you relax outside football?

'I go to good restaurants and relax at home.'

Graeme Le Saux

Blue Boy

BLUE BOY

Gustavo Poyet

Best meal:
'Uruguayan meat. Asado, like barbecue.'

Worst meal:
'I think nothing. I like all.'

Best CD:
'The Verve and Celine Dion are the last two I bought.'

Best computer game:
'Aaah. Now what do I play with my children? Doom!'

Best goal:
'My best goal? I don't remember. The most important was with Real Zaragoza when we play off to go down, and I score the first two goals and we win. We stay in the First Division and after this we win the Spanish Cup and the European Cup Winners' Cup, and this was the start of that.'

Best meal:
'Chicken and pasta.'

Worst meal:
'Vegetables. And Sian's pork chops.'

Best CD:
'The Lighthouse Family.'

Best computer game:
'Golf. Links Golf.'

Best save:
'Gordon Banks from Pelé in 1970 will never be beaten.'

Kevin Hitchcock

BLUE BOY

Best meal: 'Rice, peas and chicken, my mum's cooking.'

Worst meal: 'Any cooking that's done by Lisa and Sian upstairs in the canteen at Chelsea.'

Best CD: 'Jodeci. *Diary of a Mad Bard*.'

Best computer game: 'Track and Field.'

Best goal: 'Michael Duberry's goal, a great header, at Old Trafford. He beat two defenders, headed it past Schmeichel and ran to the ovation of 55,000 spectators. The ultimate moment!'

There was no more welcome sight in 1997–98 than Michael Duberry's return to first team action after he suffered a bad injury in January 1997 – an injury which almost certainly cost him an FA Cup Final place. After making his debut shortly before the less memorable 1994 Cup Final, the young titan did not play in the first team for over a year, but made an immediate impact in 1995–96, with strong, confident and skilful performances – culminating in the lobbed shot which hit the bar in the FA Cup semi-final of 1996. He's made up for it now with European Cup Winners' Cup and Coca-Cola Cup winner's medals.

DOOBS UNPLUGGED

If you weren't a footballer, what would you be?

'I would probably be working in a leisure centre, or something to do with sport.'

Most embarrassing moment of your life

'When I was in my second year as a YTS, David Webb called me up to join the first team at Southampton. Andy Townsend said I could lead the team out, so I ran out first. No-one else followed so I was out there by myself. All the Southampton fans must have thought: "Who's that?"'

Who do you most admire?

'Paolo Maldini (the Milan defender), the most complete player in the world.'

Advice you would give to up-and-coming youngsters:

'Just listen to whatever you're told to do and learn from others. You're never too old to learn.'

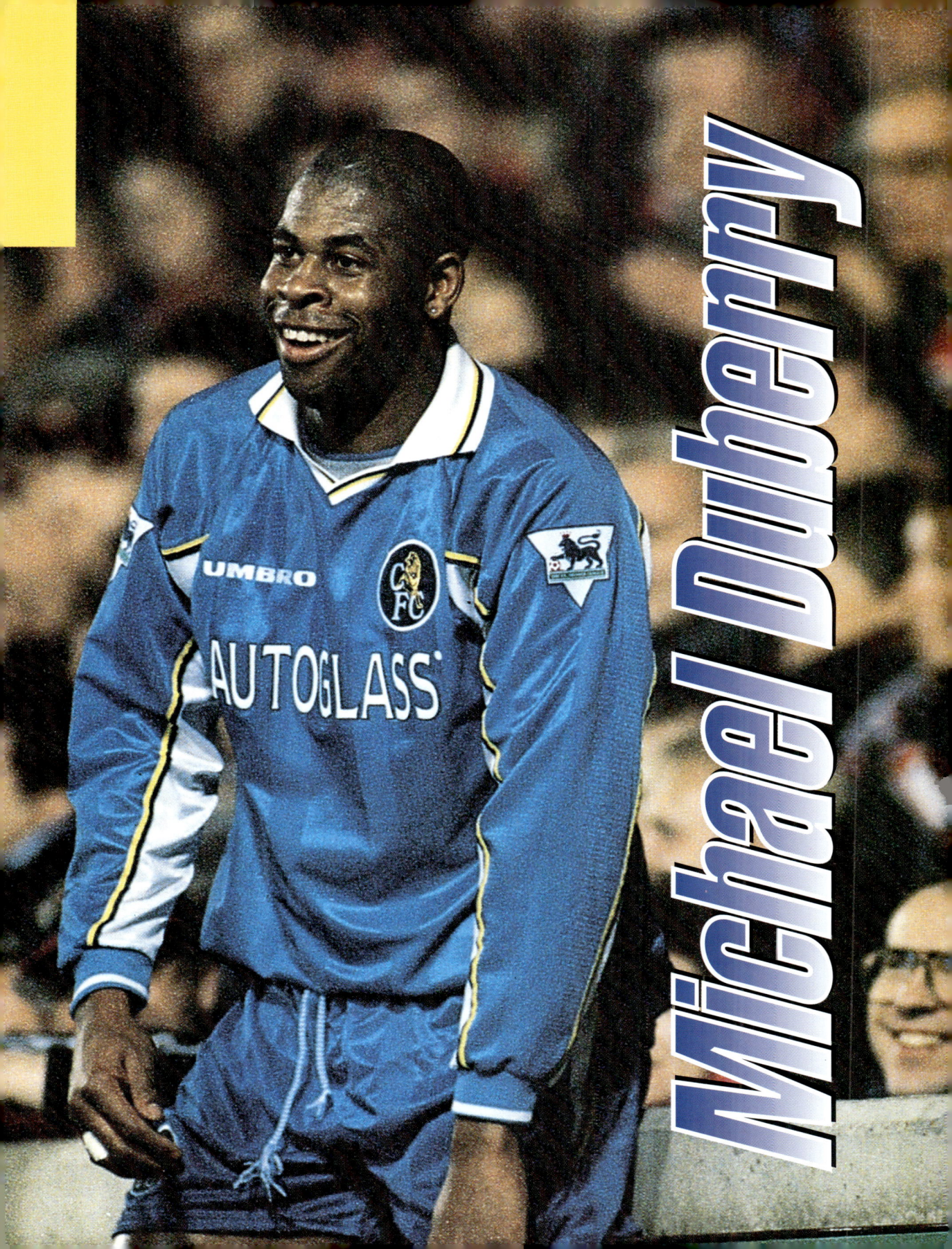

Michael Duberry

Dan Petrescu scores Chelsea's first of six at Barnsley

SIX GOALS

OR MORE

WHAT A SEASON 1997–98 turned into as Chelsea kept hammering the ball into the net. When Tore Andre Flo struck two late efforts against Crystal Palace for Chelsea's fourth 'six goals or more' haul of the campaign, he made it the third best set of sixes in Chelsea's 93-year history. It started with Gianluca Vialli getting four at Barnsley in a 6–0 trouncing, Luca got three at home to Tromsø in a 7–1 killing, then Tore Andre hit three at Tottenham in a 6–1 romp, and finally came the 6–2 win over Palace. **NOW LET'S FOLLOW THE GLORY TRAIL.**

Chelsea 6, Vialli 4, Barnsley 0
24 August 1997

Barnsley may have been poor on the day, but the Blues were unstoppable, running up their biggest ever away win in the top division. Luca Vialli, who may only have started because Mark Hughes had played for Wales midweek, thrashed four goals. His first was one of the strikes of the season.

ONE
Dan Petrescu sidefoots the first
TWO
Gustavo Poyet stabs home the second
THREE
Luca blasts home the third
FOUR
Luca half-volleys the fourth
FIVE
Luca heads home the fifth
SIX
Luca left-foots the last

‘*Vialli made me happy, he made the fans happy, he made the whole team happy.*’

Ruud Gullit

TROMSØ get a Trouncing
6 November 1997

Luca heads his hat-trick and (inset) collects the match ball

We knew they could beat us in a freezing snowstorm – and they gave us some stick afterwards. But could the Norwegian part-timers play on grass? Well, they could – but not nearly as well as the Blues. It was Luca's night. After his two goals in the first leg kept us in the tie, he scored three in the second to help Chelsea to a 7–1 win, 9–4 on aggregate.

'*I'm as happy as a baby because I couldn't remember the last time I scored at Stamford Bridge. I was desperate to score in front of my supporters who have always been great with me.*'

Gianluca Vialli

ONE
Dan Petrescu heads the first

TWO
Luca shoots low for the second

THREE
Zola smacks a free-kick home for the third

FOUR
Leboeuf pegs up another penalty for the fourth

FIVE
Luca slides in the fifth...

SIX
...and nods home the sixth

SEVEN
Dan puts us into seventh heaven

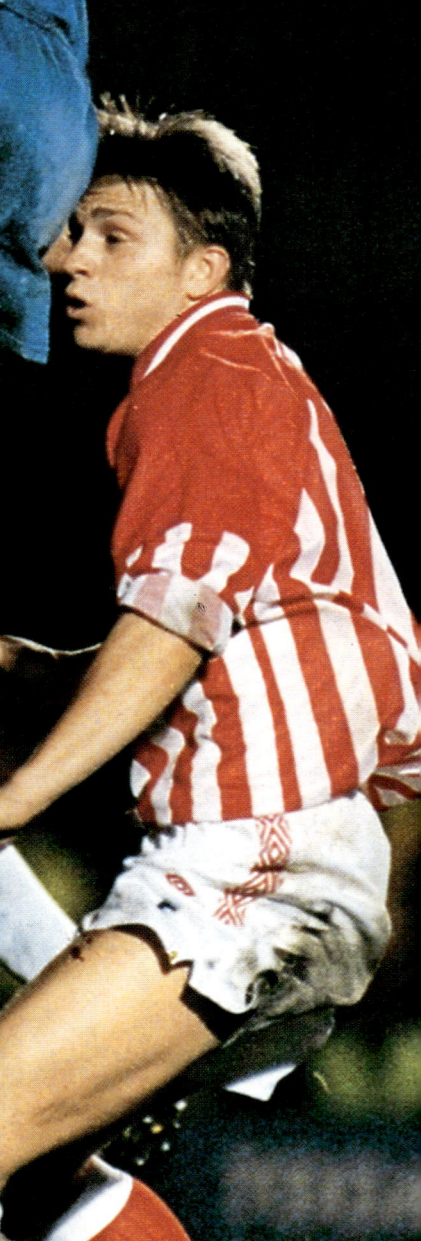

Flo heads home the first at Spurs

ONE

Flo heads in Zola's cross

TWO

Robbie Di Matteo nods in the second

THREE

Dan Petrescu flicks the third over Walker

FOUR

Flo buries the fourth

FIVE

Mark Nicholls gets his first senior goal

SIX

Flo scoops the sixth over Walker

Spurs hit for Six at White Hart Lane
6 December 1997

Tottenham must be sick of the sight of Chelsea. This all-too-easy victory took the number of meetings without defeat to 18. Chelsea went second in the table and pushed the Lilywhites into the relegation zone – a perfect day for Chelsea fans! Five goals came in the second half after Spurs had equalised just before half-time, and Tore Andre Flo scored his first hat-trick in England.

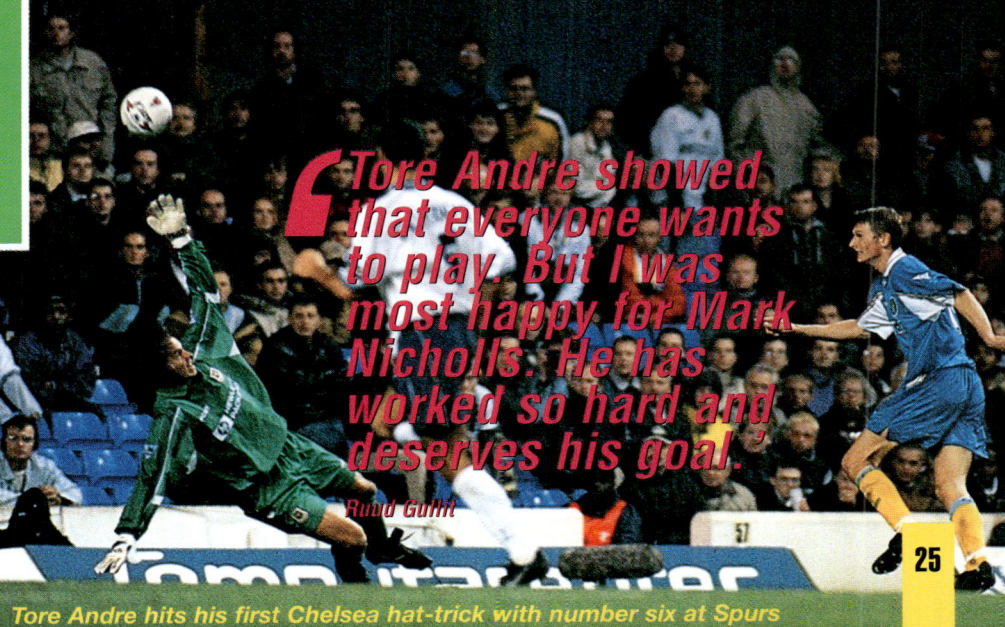

'Tore Andre showed that everyone wants to play. But I was most happy for Mark Nicholls. He has worked so hard and deserves his goal.'

Ruud Gullit

25

Tore Andre hits his first Chelsea hat-trick with number six at Spurs

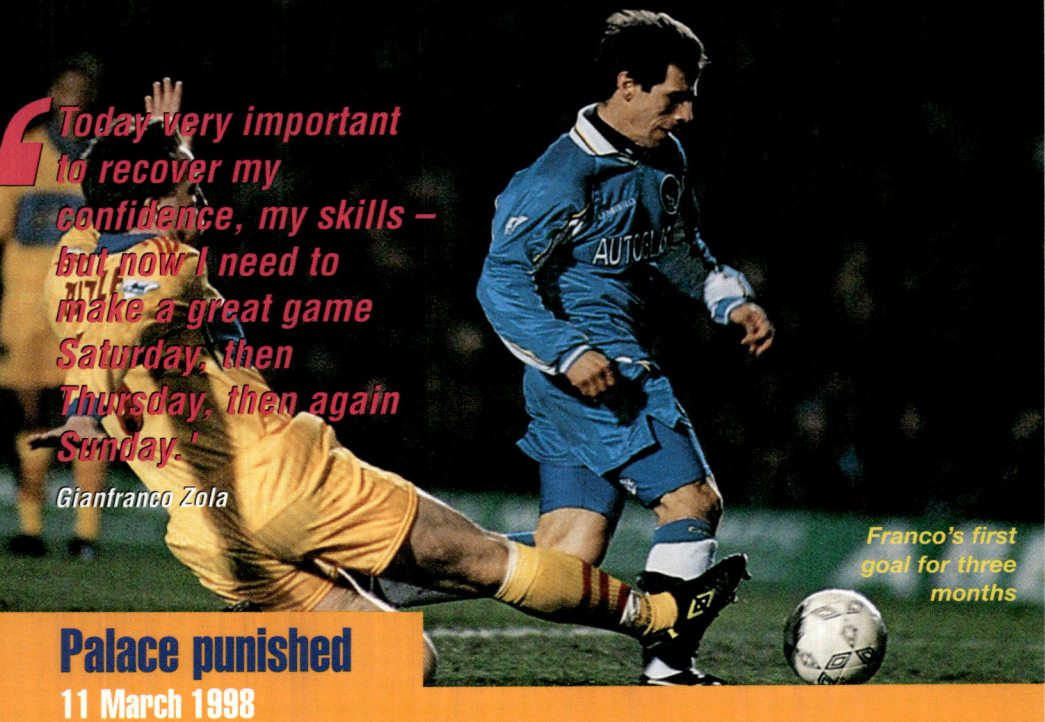

> *Today very important to recover my confidence, my skills — but now I need to make a great game Saturday, then Thursday, then again Sunday.'*
>
> *Gianfranco Zola*

Franco's first goal for three months

Palace punished
11 March 1998

Chelsea had only scored six goals in a game three times or more in a League season twice before 1997–98. First was way back in 1905–06, Chelsea's first ever campaign, when Barnsley, Blackpool, Burslem Port Vale and Clapton Orient all felt the heat. It didn't happen again until 1960–61, when Cardiff City, Newcastle (away!) and West Bromwich Albion were the victims. So, when Chelsea put six past bottom-of-the-table Crystal Palace on 11 March 1998 to add to Barnsley and Spurs, it completed a rare and remarkable achievement – all the more so since Palace had taken the lead through Hreidarsson after just six minutes.

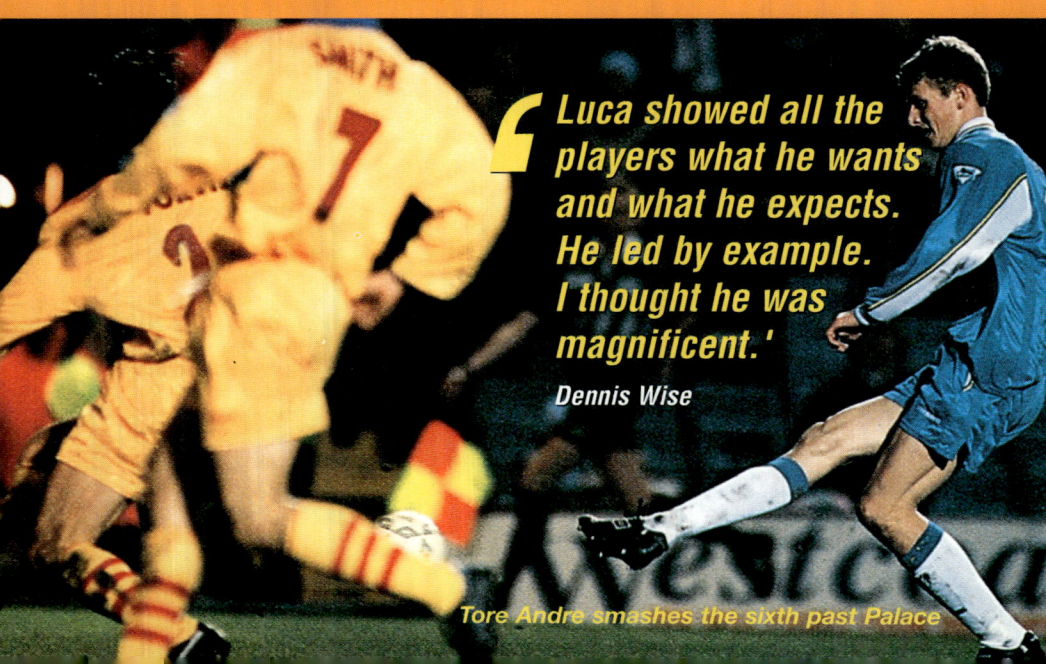

> *Luca showed all the players what he wants and what he expects. He led by example. I thought he was magnificent.'*
>
> *Dennis Wise*

Tore Andre smashes the sixth past Palace

ONE
Luca Vialli pokes home Sinclair's knockdown from Zola's corner

TWO
Gianfranco Zola takes the ball past Miller after a one-two passing movement with Vialli and slots his first goal for three months

THREE
Vialli knocks home the third after a laser-like ball from Zola and a good initial save from Miller

FOUR
A perfect pass from Zola sets Dennis Wise free inside the penalty area and he passes it into the corner to start a spree of four goals in the last seven minutes – three of them to Chelsea

FIVE
Substitute Tore Andre Flo bashes another from Petrescu's cross

SIX
Flo, again, has his initial shot saved by Miller, but the rebound breaks kindly and he puts it in

Franco's first hat-trick
29 NOVEMBER 1997

Derby had no idea how to deal with Chelsea when the Blues put on one of their most scintillating displays of the season and Italy's Gianfranco Zola scored his first hat-trick for club or country.

3

11 MINUTES
Franco takes a short pass from Robbie Di Matteo and fires the ball low into the corner from 25 yards – 1

65 MINUTES
Mart Poom in the Derby goal can't hold Mark Hughes' shot but blocks Franco's first effort from the rebound; the little Sardinian recovers to hook the ball in from an angle – 2

76 MINUTES
A perfect one-two with Di Matteo sends Franco clear and he slots home – 3

‘*The third one was the best. The action was perfect, Robbie's pass was magnificent. It was a great day.*'

Franco Zola

Franco's second against Derby

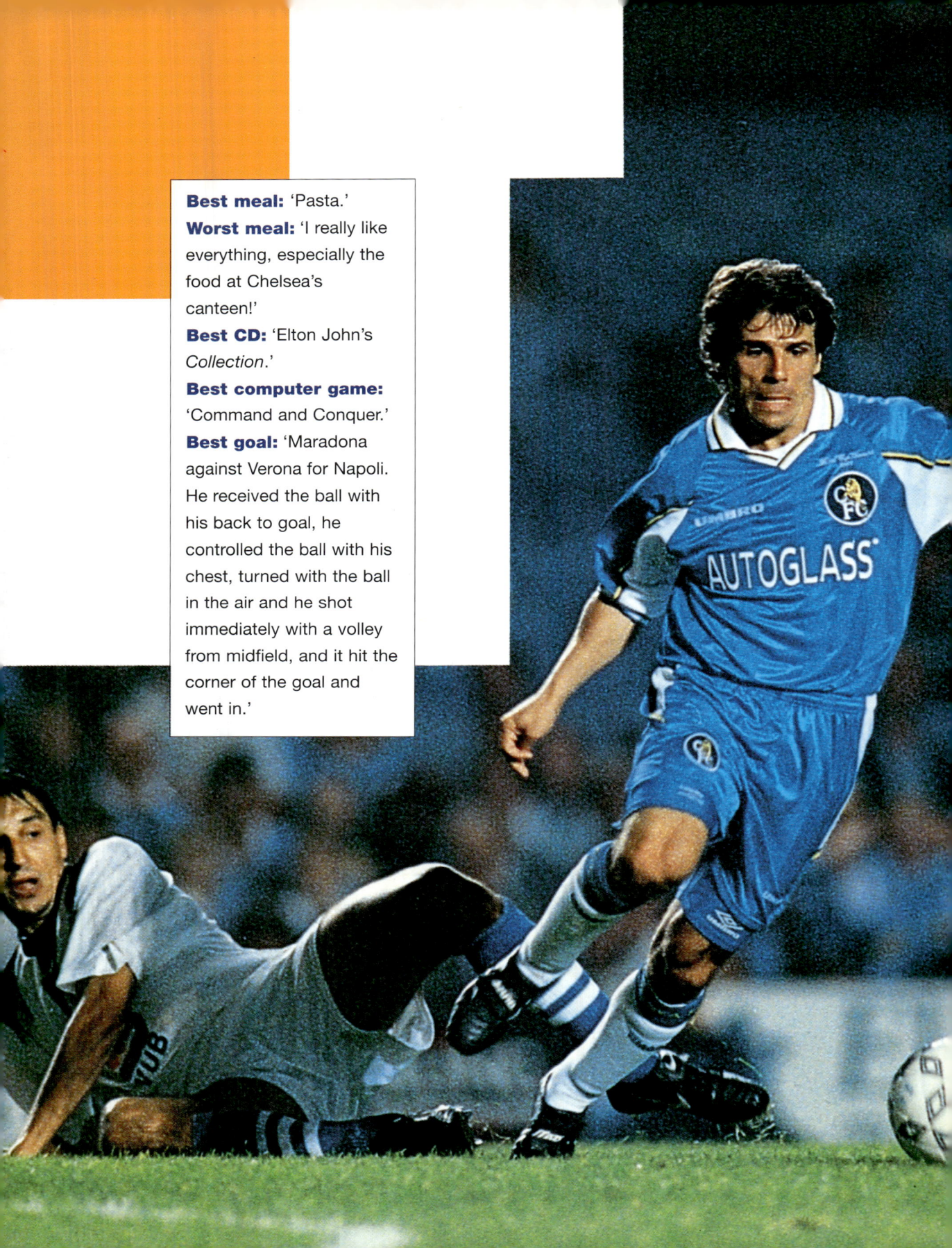

Best meal: 'Pasta.'

Worst meal: 'I really like everything, especially the food at Chelsea's canteen!'

Best CD: 'Elton John's *Collection*.'

Best computer game: 'Command and Conquer.'

Best goal: 'Maradona against Verona for Napoli. He received the ball with his back to goal, he controlled the ball with his chest, turned with the ball in the air and he shot immediately with a volley from midfield, and it hit the corner of the goal and went in.'

Incredibly, with just 30 games under his belt for Chelsea, Gianfranco Zola not only won the hearts of Blues fans but those of the whole nation and was voted Footballer of the Year in 1996-97. In 1997–98, despite the wonder goal in Stockholm, he didn't quite reach the standards he set in those incredible, unreal first six months, but what huge standards they were. Fantastic goals, moments of immense genius that won crucial games, and with it all a modest good humour that belies his superstar status. Who will forget the twisting and turning past Julian Dicks that made the hard-man defender dizzy, or the heart-stopping back-heel to himself that created the second goal against Wimbledon in the FA Cup semi-final, or the back-post back-heel that laid on a goal for Eddie Newton at Wembley? After scoring his first ever hat-trick in the 4–0 thrashing of Derby, Rams fans rose as one to clap him when he was substituted – you don't often see that these days. Forza Zola!

FRANCO UNPLUGGED

Your best goals: 'Parma against Fiorentina in the Italian Cup – we won 3–0 I think. I scored with a scissor-kick from near the penalty spot. Against Juventus one time I scored the winner five minutes from the end from a free-kick. It was a very important goal. For Chelsea I think against West Ham when we beat them 3–1 at home because it was very beautiful to see. But I think my team-mates should have warned me about Julian Dicks' reputation before the game.'

Do you still play the piano? 'I have lost a lot because I haven't played for a long time. I had lessons when I was in Naples for three years, but stopped when I went to Parma. I like to play because I find it very relaxing. I like Elton John. I'd like to be able to play all his songs but it's not possible.'

Gianfranco Zola

Eddie Newton

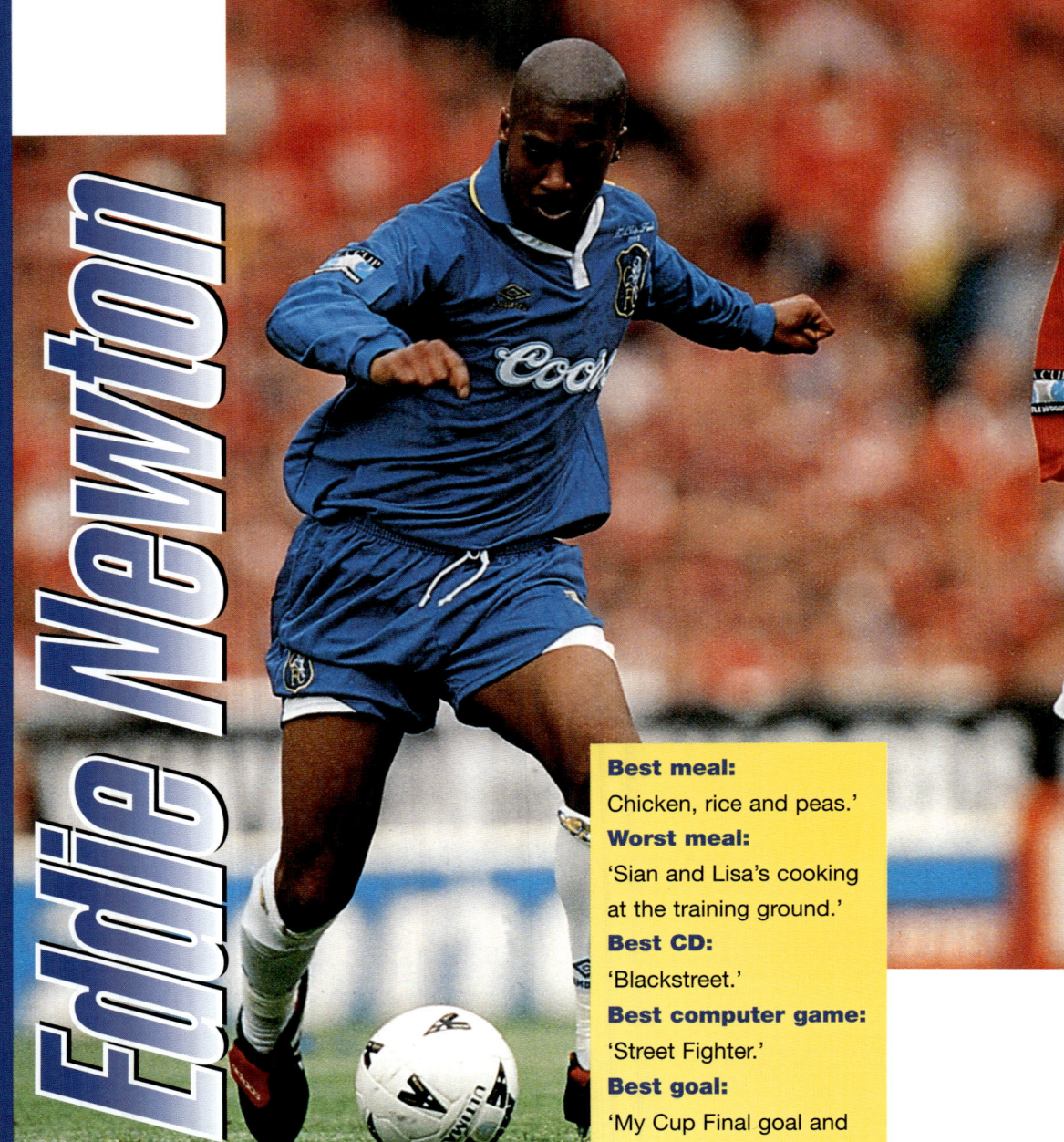

Best meal:
Chicken, rice and peas.'
Worst meal:
'Sian and Lisa's cooking at the training ground.'
Best CD:
'Blackstreet.'
Best computer game:
'Street Fighter.'
Best goal:
'My Cup Final goal and Eder's goal for Brazil against Russia in the World Cup, 1982.'

Best meal:

'Rice, peas and braising steak.'

Worst meal:

'All the cooking upstairs in the canteen at Chelsea.'

Best CD:

'Got a few. Mobb Deep. I like that gangsta rap.'

Best computer game:

'Tomb Raider II.'

Best goal:

'Roberto Carlos' free-kick against France in Le Tournoi.'

Andy Myers

BLUE BOY

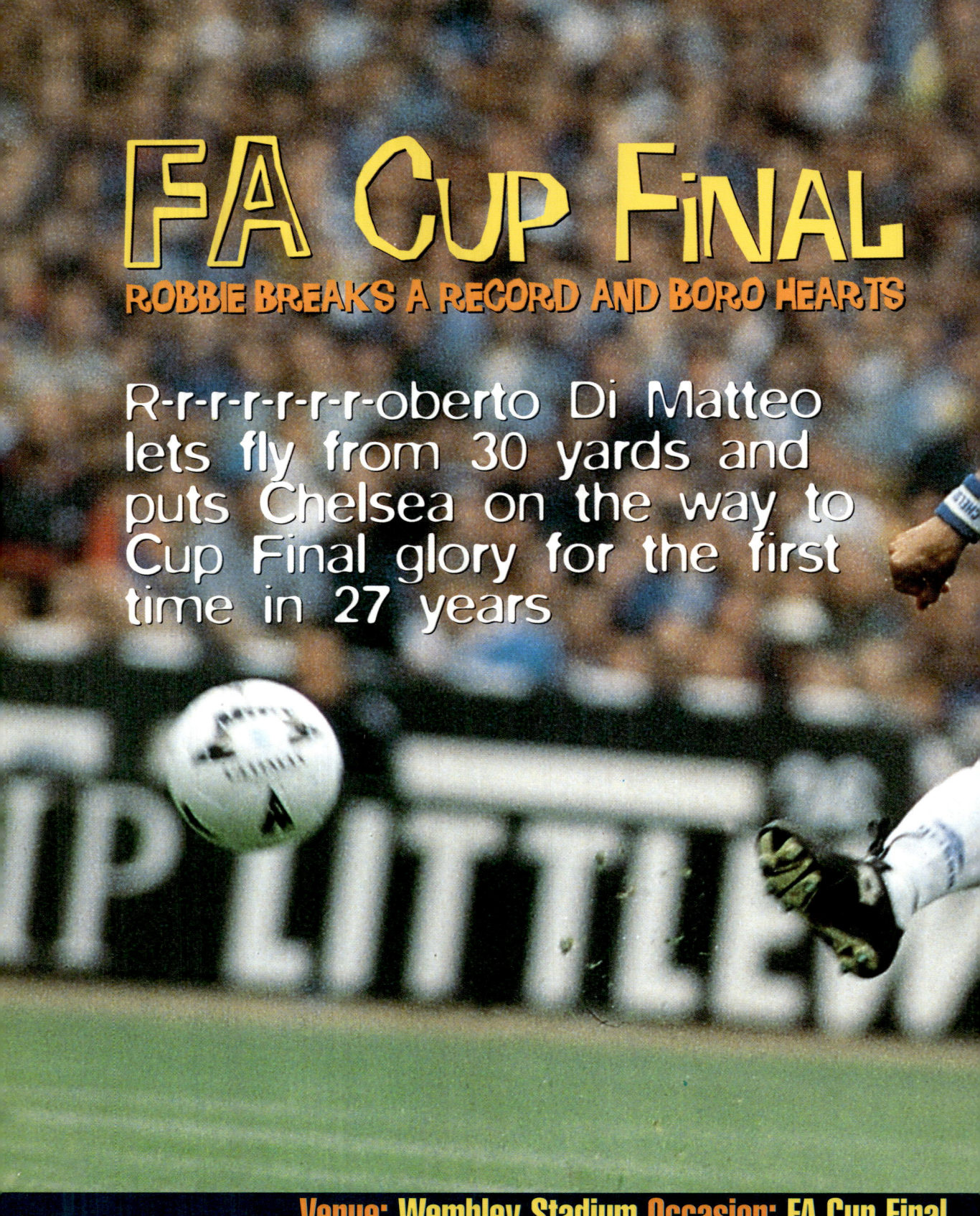

FA Cup Final

ROBBIE BREAKS A RECORD AND BORO HEARTS

R-r-r-r-r-r-oberto Di Matteo lets fly from 30 yards and puts Chelsea on the way to Cup Final glory for the first time in 27 years

Chelsea vs Middlesbrough Date: 17 May 1997 Time: 3.00:43 pm

Boro's Nigel Pearson can't stop Eddie scoring at Wembley

LOCAL BOY EDDIE MAKES IT SAFE

'It took everything out of me. I made the run, got the ball back off Zola and put it in the back of the net – and then I was celebrating. Celebrating takes a lot out of you, but you've got to do it – you don't do that too many times. But when I ran back to the halfway line I never felt so tired in all my life.'

What a time to score your first goal of the season! With eight minutes left and Chelsea nervously leading 1–0, Hammersmith-born Eddie Newton slams the ball into the Boro net. And what a goal, entirely different in its quality to Robbie's. Fourteen passes, Chelsea possession lasting 35 seconds – starting with a header from Frank Leboeuf out of defence, the ball moved swiftly from Newton to Di Matteo, to Zola and to Minto on the left wing – he hit it back to Zola, who touched it to Wisey, back to Eddie, another touch to Sinclair and one more back to Leboeuf. He played it to Wise in the centre circle, who dodged a challenge to push Eddie into space – Eddie took it forward, touched it wide right to Petrescu, whose ball to the far post was back-heeled by Zola for Eddie to score. Eight players were involved, four of them more than once, in a move from the edge of Chelsea's box to Boro's six-yard area. Simply one of the great Wembley goals.

RED DEVILS COMMIT BLUE MURDER

The joy of 17 May 1997 gave way to embarrassment as Chelsea surrendered the FA Cup at the first hurdle the following January. But what an incredible match – the Blues were truly humiliated by Manchester United, but could so easily have snatched a draw in an amazing burst of goals in the last 13 minutes. After Beckham twice, Cole twice and Sheringham had put the champions 5–0 up, Le Saux scored with a beautifully flighted chip, Vialli volleyed home the second and then grabbed the third after latching on to Pallister's poor pass back. Di Matteo had shot just wide after the second Chelsea goal – if that had gone in, an incredible escape might have happened.

'You can't concede so many goals to a big team like Manchester United. We gave our best, but it wasn't enough.'
Roberto Di Matteo

Two-goal Cole is foiled on this occasion by a last-ditch Steve Clarke tackle

Best meal:

'Chicken and rice by my mum.'

Worst meal:

'Indian. I don't like Indian food.'

Best CD:

'Chico Debarge.'

Best computer game:

'I'm not into computers.'

Best goal:

'One against Southampton, a 3–0 win at home. Ruudi and Sparky scored later, but I took a pass from Wisey, controlled it, took it down and beat Bez [Dave Beasant] in the bottom left-hand corner.'

FRANK UNPLUGGED

Most memorable childhood game:

'Playing for Chelsea under-13s away at Arsenal. It was the same day John Hollins got sacked. Gwyn Williams was in charge of us but got called away. He left the parents in charge and told them to play me in midfield but I insisted they play me up front. We beat them 3–2 and I scored a hat-trick. Gwyn gave me some stick when he found out.'

Chelsea have in recent years put out the occasional team featuring ten internationals and Frank Sinclair has often been the odd man out. Not any more! The fast and determined full-back put his Jamaican roots to good use and gave himself the chance to go to the World Cup with the Reggae Boyz – and who would deny him the pleasure? In the first team since 1991, Frank was Player of the Year in 1993, played left-back in the 1994 Cup Final (giving away the second, very debatable penalty) then played right-back at Wembley in 1997. Injuries have been a problem for him in recent years, but he scored the first goal of the 1997–98 campaign, an important one against Real Betis in the Cup Winners' Cup, and just keeps storming back into contention.

Frank Sinclair

Jody Morris

Best meal:
'Fry up.'

Worst meal:
'Quiche.'

Best CD:
'The Notorious BIG.'

Best computer game:
'Championship Manager.'

Best goal:
'Mine against Southampton in the Coca-Cola Cup, extra time, just because it was in the first team and at home.'

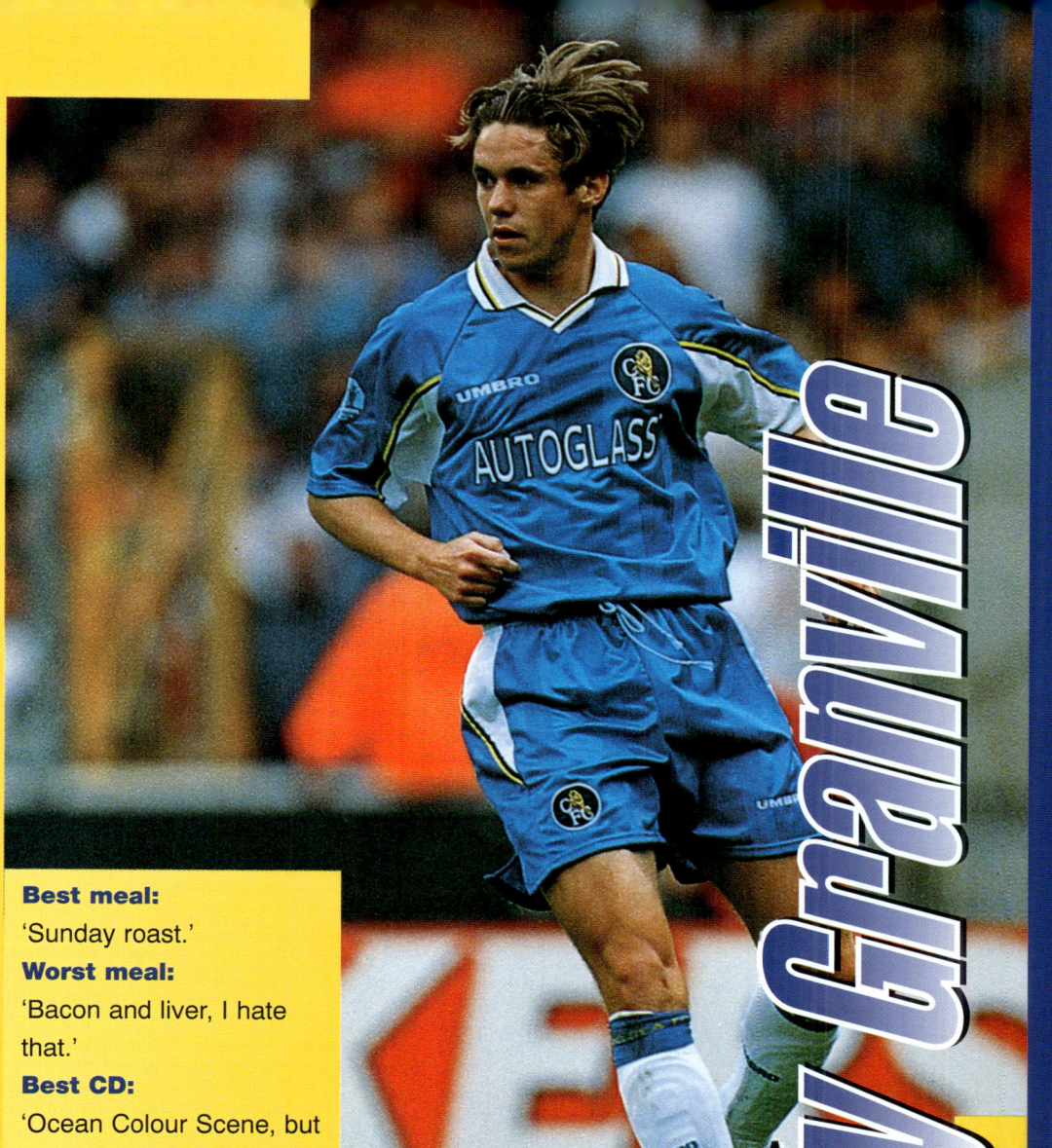

BLUE BOY

Danny Granville

Best meal:
'Sunday roast.'

Worst meal:
'Bacon and liver, I hate that.'

Best CD:
'Ocean Colour Scene, but my brother's band Reece is going to be big.'

Best computer game:
'Fifa '98.'

Best goal:
'I saw Marco Van Basten do an overhead kick for Milan, and that's got to be it. That's second behind mine against Slovan Bratislava.'

Mark Hughes

Best meal:

'My wife's sweet and sour chicken.'

Worst meal:

'Anything with cabbage.'

Best CD:

'*Unforgettable Fire* by U2.'

Best computer game:

'Ridge Racer.'

Best goal:

'Terry Phelan's for Manchester City against Tottenham in the Cup. A great goal. And I don't think many players will choose that one!'

'Sparky' came to Stamford Bridge aged 31, a Manchester United cast-off as Alex Ferguson gave youth a go at Old Trafford – but in three seasons down south he has proved to be far from finished. So much so that in 1997 he became the first player to win four FA Cup winner's medals this century – surely no-one else can do it before the new millennium begins – and was Chelsea's Player of the Year when Gianfranco Zola was busy winning all the plaudits and the Footballer of the Year award. Another one the opposing fans love to loathe, Mark will be 35 in November 1998, but who would bet against him playing on for a while yet?

HUGHESY UNPLUGGED

Best subject at school:

'Surprisingly, English!'

Do you still support the team you did when you were young?

'No, they support me! I've always been a Chelsea supporter.'

Most prized possession as a teenager:

'A pair of football boots I won at a raffle. I never thought I would win them. My ticket number was 1, so it was meant to be.'

Posters you hung on the wall when you were young:

'The pop groups Blondie and The Jam.'

Song which got everyone on to the dance floor at school discos:

'"Under the Moon of Love" by Showaddywaddy. That makes me feel really old!'

Best meal: 'Spaghetti with seafood.'

Worst meal: 'Burgers.'

Best CD: 'The Spice Girls.'

Best computer game: 'I don't play computer games.'

Best goal: 'Maradona against England, and Weah for Milan against Verona – he started from his own corner and flew all the way through.'

Dan Petrescu, known by team-mates as 'Ledge' (the legend), came to Chelsea for £2.3m in November 1995, a proven international who'd had an unhappy time at Sheffield Wednesday. In his native Romania he'd won four League Championships and two Romanian FA Cups with Steaua Bucharest, and had also played in Italy with Foggia and Genoa. As a right wing-back he was perfectly designed for the five-at-the-back system favoured by Glenn Hoddle, but has put in some sterling performances pushed forward into midfield as tactics changed under Gullit and Vialli. Perhaps his best performance was in the supercharged atmosphere of the FA Cup tie against Liverpool in January 1997 when he just kept popping up out of nowhere and laid on the crucial third goal for Luca as Chelsea won 4–2 from 0–2 down.

'LEDGE' UNPLUGGED

Best player you have played with or against:

'Maradona. I played against him when he played for Argentina and Napoli. Every time he touched the ball he was the best.'

Highest point in your career:

'Scoring in the 1994 World Cup against the USA. It was the last group game and we qualified with my goal.'

Lowest point:

'Missing a penalty in the shoot-out against Switzerland in the World Cup quarter-finals, 1994.'

Favourite hobbies outside football:

'Playing and watching tennis, watching rugby and movies.'

Team you support:

'Chelsea and Steaua Bucharest.'

Dan Patrescu

QUICK QUIZ

Pit your wits against these brain-twisting teasers

A ANAGRAMS

Here are some anagrams of players' names. Can you work out who they are?

1 Thick oven chick
2 Boo, me editor tart
3 Rachel, turn a vet
4 Clever steak
5 M randy? Yes
6 O Ken, a bluffer
7 Di went on Dee
8 I rank him tried
9 Er, fool ranted
10 Wines, dines
11 E, crude pants
12 Dee, library chum
13 Grain? FA zoo clan
14 A large sex emu

B SPELL CHECK

Who comes up as the following on the computer spell check?

1 Eddy Dame Gory
2 Giant-luck Villain
3 Deny Granule
4 Dents Wales
5 Joy Morose
6 Pole Huggers
7 Greasy Leg Sax
8 Stiff Clare
9 Handy Driers
10 Gin France Cola

C WHO...?

1. Who's the shortest of these four?
a) Dennis Wise
b) Jody Morris
c) Gianfranco Zola
d) Tore Andre Flo

2. Who's the tallest of these four?
a) Michael Duberry
b) Bernard Lambourde
c) Frank Leboeuf
d) Dan Petrescu

3. Who weighs the most of these four?
a) David Lee
b) Frank Sinclair
c) Andy Myers
d) Mark Hughes

4. Who's the oldest of these four?
a) Danny Granville
b) Roberto Di Matteo
c) Dmitri Kharine
d) Gustavo Poyet

5. Who's the youngest of these four?
a) Ed de Goey
b) Gianluca Vialli
c) Dennis Wise
d) Kevin Hitchcock

6. Who made his Chelsea debut first of these four?
a) David Rocastle
b) Andy Myers
c) Jody Morris
d) Graeme Le Saux

D WHAT...?

1 ...did Chelsea do in season 1990–91 that no-one else could do?

2 ...did Chelsea do in season 1993–94 that no-one else could do?

3 ...did Gianfranco Zola win in 1996–97 that no other Chelsea player has won?

4 ...big thing did Ed de Goey become when he signed for Chelsea?

5 ...is the name of Frank Leboeuf's wife?

6 ...international medal did Celestine Babayaro win in 1996?

7 ...is Tore Andre Flo's ex-Sheffield United brother called?

8 ...happened to Ken Monkou in his last match for Chelsea?

9 ...was special about Scott Minto's last game for Chelsea?

10 ...landmark did Chelsea reach when Gianfranco Zola scored the third goal against Real Betis at the Bridge on 19 March 1998?

Answers

A ANAGRAMS
1 Kevin Hitchcock
2 Roberto Di Matteo
3 Laurent Charvet
4 Steve Clarke
5 Andy Myers
6 Frank Leboeuf
7 Eddie Newton
8 Dmitri Kharine
9 Tore Andre Flo
10 Dennis Wise
11 Dan Petrescu
12 Michael Duberry
13 Gianfranco Zola
14 Graeme Le Saux

B SPELL CHECK
1 Ed de Goey
2 Gianluca Vialli
3 Danny Granville
4 Dennis Wise
5 Jody Morris
6 Paul Hughes
7 Graeme Le Saux
8 Steve Clarke
9 Andy Myers
10 Gianfranco Zola

C WHO...?
1. Jody Morris, 5ft 5in.
2. Bernard Lambourde, 6ft 2in.
3. David Lee, 95.5kg.
4. Gustavo Poyet, born 15 November 1967.
5. Ed de Goey, born 20 December 1966.
6. Graeme Le Saux, 13 May 1989.

D WHAT
1 Beat champions Arsenal in the League (they only lost one game all season).
2 The League double over champions Manchester United.
3 The Footballer of the Year award.
4 Chelsea's tallest ever player at 6ft 6in.
5 Betty.
6 The Olympic gold medal for football with Nigeria.
7 Jostein.
8 He was sent off at Everton in May 1992 for cuffing Peter Beardsley over the head.
9 It was the glorious 1997 FA Cup Final.
10 It was the Blues' 100th goal in European competition.

Ask any top football manager what he needs to have a successful team and one of the things he'll tell you is a strong squad of players. Last season, both Ruud Gullit and Gianluca Vialli took full advantage of Chelsea's talented squad whose names are listed below.

These names appear in the wordsearch grid in the usual way: across, down or diagonally, either forwards or backwards, in a straight uninterrupted line. We've marked one as a starter to give you the right idea.

Cross them off the list as you find them and you'll discover that we've been a bit sneaky: ONE NAME DOESN'T APPEAR IN THE GRID AT ALL! Can you work out which player is missing? Turn to page 46 for the solution.

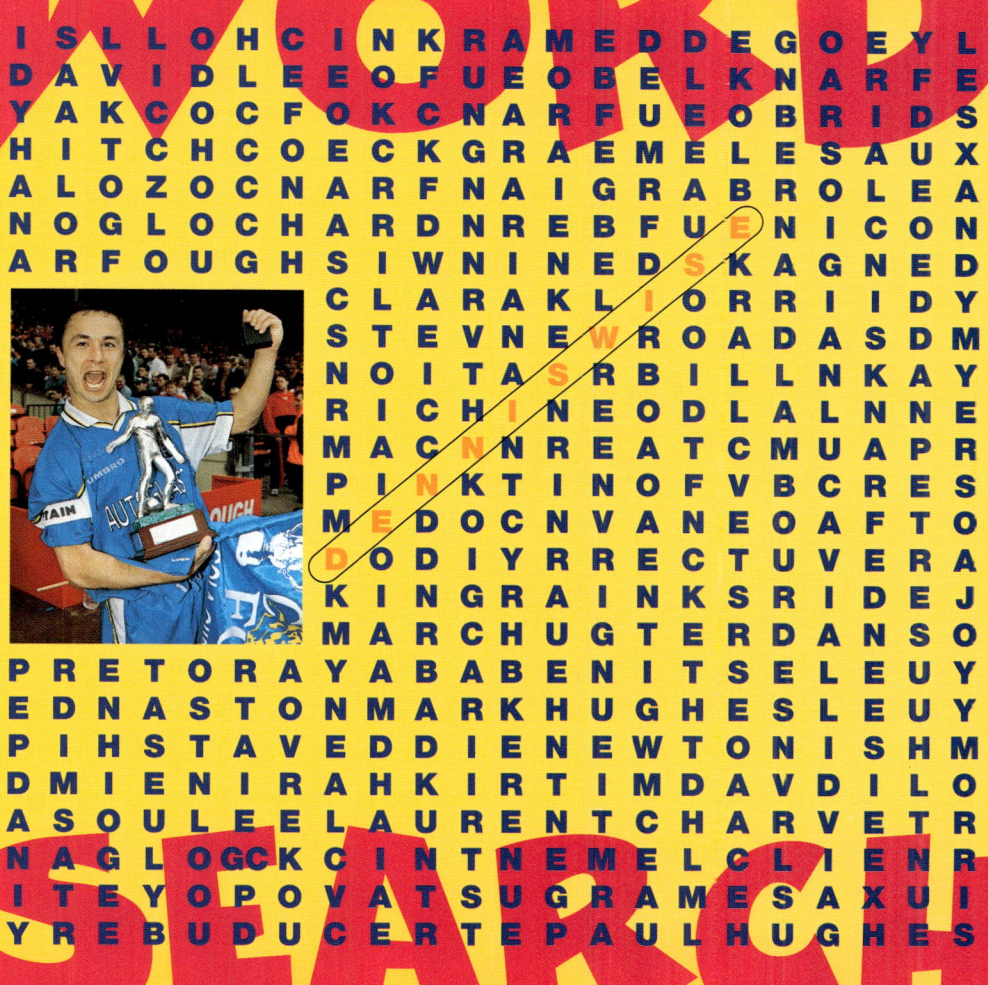

```
I S L L O H C I N K R A M E D D E G O E Y L
D A V I D L E E O F U E O B E L K N A R F E
Y A K C O C F O K C N A R F U E O B R I D S
H I T C H C O E C K G R A E M E L E S A U X
A L O Z O C N A R F N A I G R A B R O L E A
N O G L O C H A R D N R E B F U E N I C O N
A R F O U G H S I W N I N E D S K A G N E D
    C L A R A K L I O R R I I D Y
    S T E V N E W R O A D A S D M
    N O I T A S R B I L L N K A Y
    R I C H I N E O D L A L N N E
    M A C N N R E A T C M U A P R
    P I N K T I N O F V B C R E S
    M E D O C N V A N E O A F T O
    D O D I Y R R E C T U V E R A
    K I N G R A I N K S R I D E J
    M A R C H U G T E R D A N S O
P R E T O R A Y A B A B E N I T S E L E U Y
E D N A S T O N M A R K H U G H E S L E U Y
P I H S T A V E D D I E N E W T O N I S H M
D M I E N I R A H K I R T I M D A V D I L O
A S O U L E E L A U R E N T C H A R V E T R
N A G L O G C K C I N T N E M E L C L I E N R
I T E Y O P O V A T S U G R A M E S A X U I
Y R E B U D U C E R T E P A U L H U G H E S
```

ANDY MYERS
BERNARD LAMBOURDE
CELESTINE BABAYARO
DAN PETRESCU
DANNY GRANVILLE
DAVID LEE
DENNIS WISE
DMITRI KHARINE

ED DE GOEY
EDDIE NEWTON
FRANK LEBOEUF
FRANK SINCLAIR
GIANFRANCO ZOLA
GIANLUCA VIALLI
GRAEME LE SAUX
GUSTAVO POYET

JODY MORRIS
KEVIN HITCHCOCK
LAURENT CHARVET
MARK HUGHES
MARK NICHOLLS
MICHAEL DUBERRY
NEIL CLEMENT
NICK COLGAN

NICK CRITTENDEN
PAUL HUGHES
ROBERTO DI MATTEO
STEVE CLARKE
TORE ANDRE FLO

solution see page 46

45

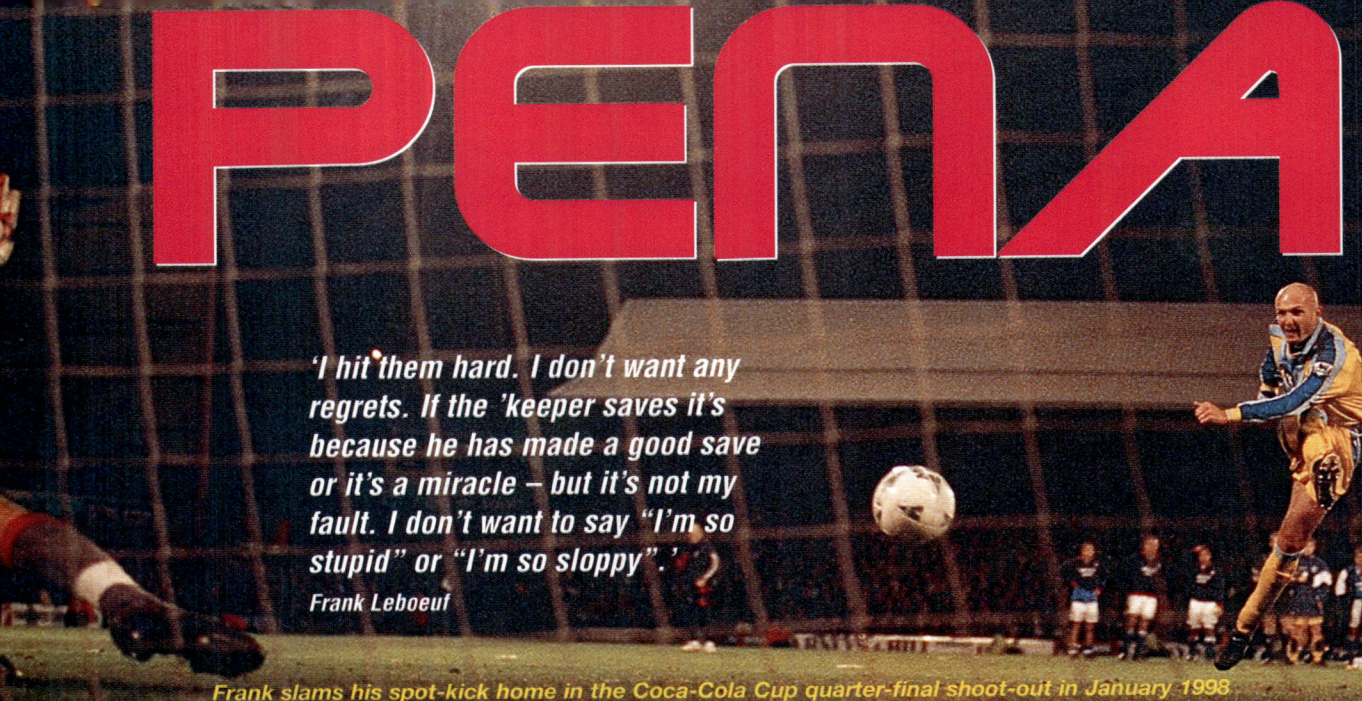

PENA

'I hit them hard. I don't want any regrets. If the 'keeper saves it's because he has made a good save or it's a miracle – but it's not my fault. I don't want to say "I'm so stupid" or "I'm so sloppy".'
Frank Leboeuf

Frank slams his spot-kick home in the Coca-Cola Cup quarter-final shoot-out in January 1998

FRANK'S ALWAYS ON THE SPOT

PRESSURE: 'At Strasbourg against Bordeaux it was 1–1 in the 91st minute, with the stadium completely full. We had a penalty. I slipped just before, but put it just under the crossbar. It was perfect. I scored a free-kick just before. It was my day.'

ADVICE TO KIDS: 'Choose a side; don't change – never; and shoot strongest you can.'

A quick look up and **BANG**, it's in the back of the net – plenty of welly and little fuss. Just another Frank Leboeuf penalty kick.

'I have to concede that when I was young, I missed every one,' says Frank. 'When I arrived at Laval, my first team, there was already someone who took them. When he left I took his place and I didn't miss one. Then in five years at Strasbourg I missed two or three. They were saved – I never shoot outside the goal. At Chelsea it has worked very well, but you never know. Sometimes you can miss – you don't know why. You need a lot of luck.'

Frank rarely practises: 'If I do, I shoot just one, because it's like the real thing. It's a question of mentality.'

(solution to word search - STEVE CLARKE)

FACING THE PENALTY

Ed de Goey was beaten by five great penalties in the Charity Shield in August 1997, but made two superb saves at Ipswich in January to take Chelsea to the Coca-Cola Cup semi-finals, flinging out an arm to deny Scowcroft, then stopping Taricco's weak spot-kick. 'I think my best save was the first one at Ipswich,' says Ed. 'It was very far in the corner; I just went at full length and saved it with one hand.'

Penalty shoot-outs decided four matches for the Blues in 1997-98 and they won three of them. One of those was in the pre-season Umbro Cup against Newcastle, the other two came in the Coca-Cola Cup – Chelsea beat Blackburn in the third round 4–1, then dumped Ipswich by the same score in the quarter-final.

Kevin Hitchcock was in goal against Blackburn in October and brilliantly palmed away Chris Sutton's powerful penalty, then watched as Lars Bohinen chipped the ball over his bar. 'Chris Sutton hit a good pen, but it was at a nice height,' says Kevin. 'When I saved the first one, the second one was a bit of pressure for them.'

'I love penalty shoot-outs. It's a battle of wits. You pick your side and then you go all out to put something in the way of the ball.'

'You wait as long as possible and just go, and maybe you have a little luck.'

Ed guesses right to keep out Taricco's weak kick in the Coca-Cola Cup quarter-finals

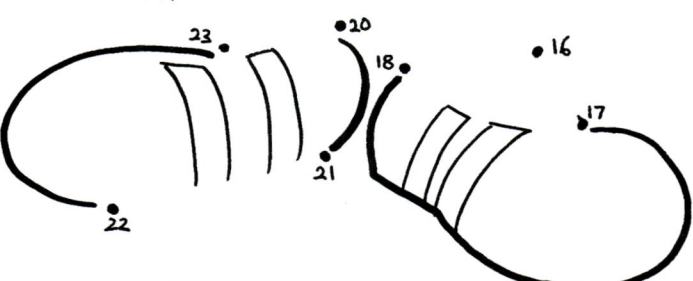

JOIN THE DOTS

SPOT THE DIFFERENCE

Wisey's cooking up some trouble in Robbie's restaurant, with the help of Franco, Eddie Newton, Gustavo, Frank Sinclair, Frank Leboeuf and Luca. Can you spot ten differences between the two pictures?

Answers on page 51

400 up and still going strong

STEVE CLARKE FACTFILE

Born: Saltcoats, Ayrshire, 29 August 1963

Previous club: St Mirren

Signed: January 1987 for £422,000

Blues debut: 24 January 1987, against Norwich (a) as substitute for David Speedie – drew 2–2

Honours: European Cup Winners' Cup winner's medal 1998, FA Cup winner's medal 1997, runners-up medal 1994, Coca-Cola Cup winner's medal 1998, Second Division championship medal 1989, Player of the Year 1994, St Mirren Player of the Year 1986

Chelsea goals: ten

International caps: six full Scotland caps (all won while at Chelsea), two Scotland B caps (both won while at Chelsea), eight Scotland under-21 caps. Represented Football League against Rest of the World, August 1987, at Wembley

Milestones: 100th first team appearance vs Leicester (a), 15 April 1989 (lost 0–2); 200th first team appearance vs Sheffield Wednesday (a), 22 August 1992 (drew 3–3); 300th first team appearance vs Real Zaragoza, European Cup Winners' Cup semi-final, 6 April 1985 (lost 0–3); 400th first team appearance vs Ipswich Town (a), 7 January 1998 as substitute for Frank Sinclair (drew 2–2, won penalty shoot-out 4–1)

Long-serving defender Steve Clarke created history in January 1998 when he joined a select band of Blues who have played 400 games for the club. Only the eighth player to reach this extraordinary milestone, Clarkey is typically modest about his achievement: 'I don't think you ever set out to stay 11 years with one club. To be honest it doesn't really feel as if I've passed 400 games and it doesn't mean that much to me at the moment. I just want to get as many appearances in as I can – when my career's over I can look back on it and say that was quite an achievement.'

BEST MEMORIES

'The 1993–94 season when I got Player of the Year, that meant a lot to me – and winning the FA Cup. They were probably the two highlights of the 11 years.'

The 400 Club

1. **Ron Harris (1961–80) – 795.** The legendary defender's record is unlikely to be broken.
2. **Peter Bonetti (1959–79) – 729.** The Cat's athleticism brought goalkeeping into the modern era.
3. **John Hollins (1963–75 & 1983–84) – 592.** Midfield dynamo who later managed the club.

4. **Steve Clarke (1987–98) – 421 at the end of 1997-98.**
5. **Kerry Dixon (1983–92) – 420.** Goalscoring machine who heartbreakingly missed setting a new Blues goals record by 10 strikes.
6. **Eddie McCreadie (1962–74) – 410.** Nicknamed Clarence after the short-sighted lion in children's adventure programme *Daktari*, the extravagant full-back managed the club to promotion in 1977.
7. **John Bumstead (1978–92) – 409.** 'Bummers' just went on and on in midfield.
8. **Ken Armstrong (1946–57) – 402.** Championship-winning wing-half.

Answers to *Spot the Difference*
The ten differences are: Gustavo's serving dish; Gustavo's bow tie; Frank Sinclair's scarf; Robbie's cuff-link; Robbie's carnation; Wisey's spoon; the frying pan hanging up; Frank Leboeuf's chef's hat; Luca's button; and the onion on the table.

Wise Heads On

Dennis Wise Factfile

Born: Kensington, 16 December 1966

Previous clubs: Southampton, Wimbledon

Signed: July 1990 for £1.6 million, then a club record

Blues debut: 25 August 1990, against Derby County (h). Chelsea won 2–1

Honours: European Cup Winners' Cup winner's medal 1998, FA Cup winner's medal 1997, runners-up medal 1994, Coca-Cola Cup winner's medal 1998; also an FA Cup winner's medal in 1988 with Wimbledon and Wimbledon Player of the Year 1988

Chelsea goals: 61, including 18 penalties

International caps: 12 full England caps (all won at Chelsea), one goal; three England B caps, one goal; one England under-21 cap

Milestones: 100th appearance vs Walsall (h), Coca-Cola Cup, 7 October 1992 (won 1–0); 200th appearance vs Newcastle United (a), 24 September 1995 (lost 0–2); 300th appearance vs Ipswich Town (a), Coca-Cola Cup, 7 January 1998 (drew 2-2, won penalty shoot-out 4–1)

The 26th player to make 300 appearances for the Blues, Wisey was just the third Chelsea captain to lift a major trophy for the club, after Roy Bentley (Championship 1955) and Ron Harris (FA Cup 1970, European Cup Winners' Cup 1971). He is also the only player currently with the Blues to have scored more than 50 goals for them.

BEST MEMORY OF FIRST 300 GAMES
'Obviously winning the FA Cup, and lifting it, was the highlight. And I'm proud that all my 12 England caps have been won while I've been with Chelsea.'

Charity Shield Chelsea vs Manchester United, 3 August 1997

HUGHES SHOWS UNITED NO CHARITY

Mark Hughes wriggled free of his marker to head home the first goal in the 1997 Charity Shield, traditional curtain-raiser to the season, showing no qualms about putting one past former team-mate Peter Schmeichel. His first cuddle came from debut man Gustavo Poyet who turned into an instant hit with the Blues fans. In a bad-tempered game, neither side dominated and it was down to penalties – not for the last time in the 1997-98 season.

Schmeichel saved Frank Sinclair's spot-kick and Robbie Di Matteo blasted over. United scored four and took the Charity Shield home again.

'To lose by penalties I don't mind so much because it is a lottery. From our point of view it was a festival of bad passing, bad mistakes.'

Ruud Gullit

If he had only ever played that one game for Chelsea, the FA Cup Final of 1997, his name would be hallowed at Stamford Bridge forever for his 43-second strike of strikes. Nine goals in his first season after arriving from Italy's Lazio for £4.9 million was Robbie's best return for any club, and startling because he was used to playing the anchor role in midfield. He bettered with ten goals in 1997-98.

He looks strangely lazy on the pitch and can seem to disappear from games, only to emerge and do something wonderful, even match-winning – remember his solo effort at home to Real Betis? Smooth, skilful and with the sound positional sense that some Italian footballers seem to be born with, baby-faced Robbie is also the celebration king of Stamford Bridge.

Best meal: 'Mama's pasta, of course.'

Worst meal: 'Tripe. I can't eat that. Maybe it's the only food I can't eat.'

Best CD: 'Simple Minds, double album. The black one.'

Best computer game: 'I've never played with a computer.'

Best goal: 'The Cup Final, of course!'

ROBBIE UNPLUGGED

Most memorable childhood game:

'I was playing for Schaffhausen against Zurich in Switzerland when I was eight years old. We won 21–0 and I scored about 16 goals. My father was watching the game and every time I scored he picked up a stone so he wouldn't lose count.'

Room-mate abroad:

'Demetrio Albertini. He's a nice guy and looks after me. We are interested in the same things.'

Worst room-mate to share with:

'Luca. You cannot move, breathe, sneeze. You cannot make any noise because he wants silence.'

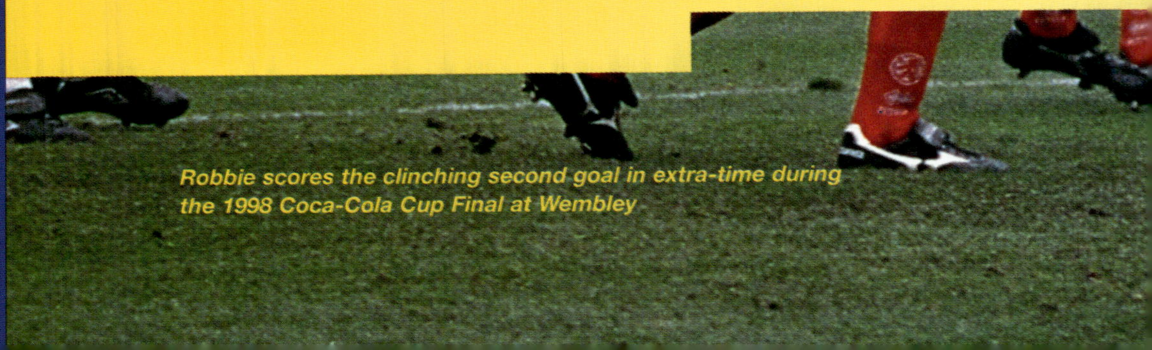

Robbie scores the clinching second goal in extra-time during the 1998 Coca-Cola Cup Final at Wembley

Roberto Di Matteo

BLUE BOY

Celestine Babayaro

Best meal:

'Rice and beans.'

Worst meal:

'I eat anything man, except… pork!'

Best CD:

'Boyz 2 Men.'

Best computer game:

'I don't play computer games.'

Best goal:

'Against Argentina in the Olympic Final, my header, and I won the gold medal.'

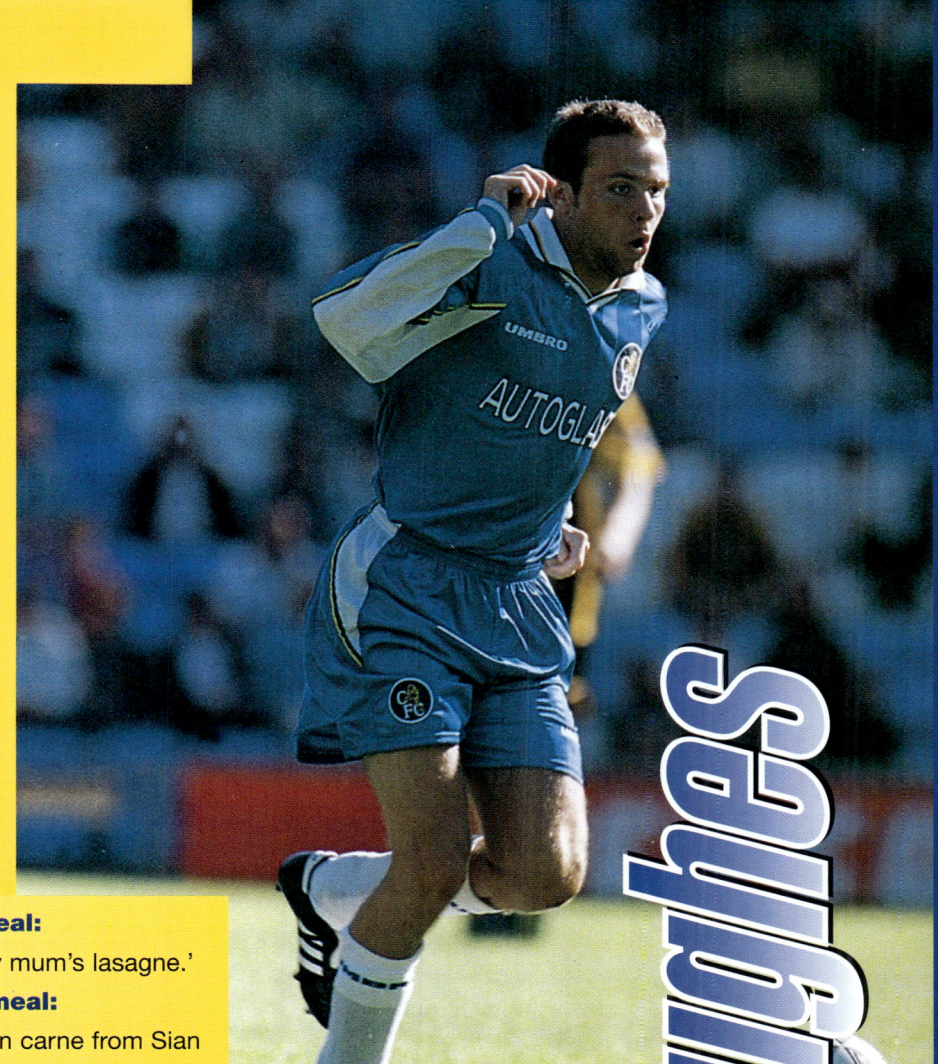

Paul Hughes

Best meal:

'I like my mum's lasagne.'

Worst meal:

'Chilli con carne from Sian and Lisa at the training ground.'

Best CD:

'George Michael, *Older*.'

Best computer game:

'Fifa '98 and Tomb Raider II.'

Best goal:

'Clarence Seedorf for Real Madrid pinged it from just inside his own half, or Roberto Carlos from the corner flag.'

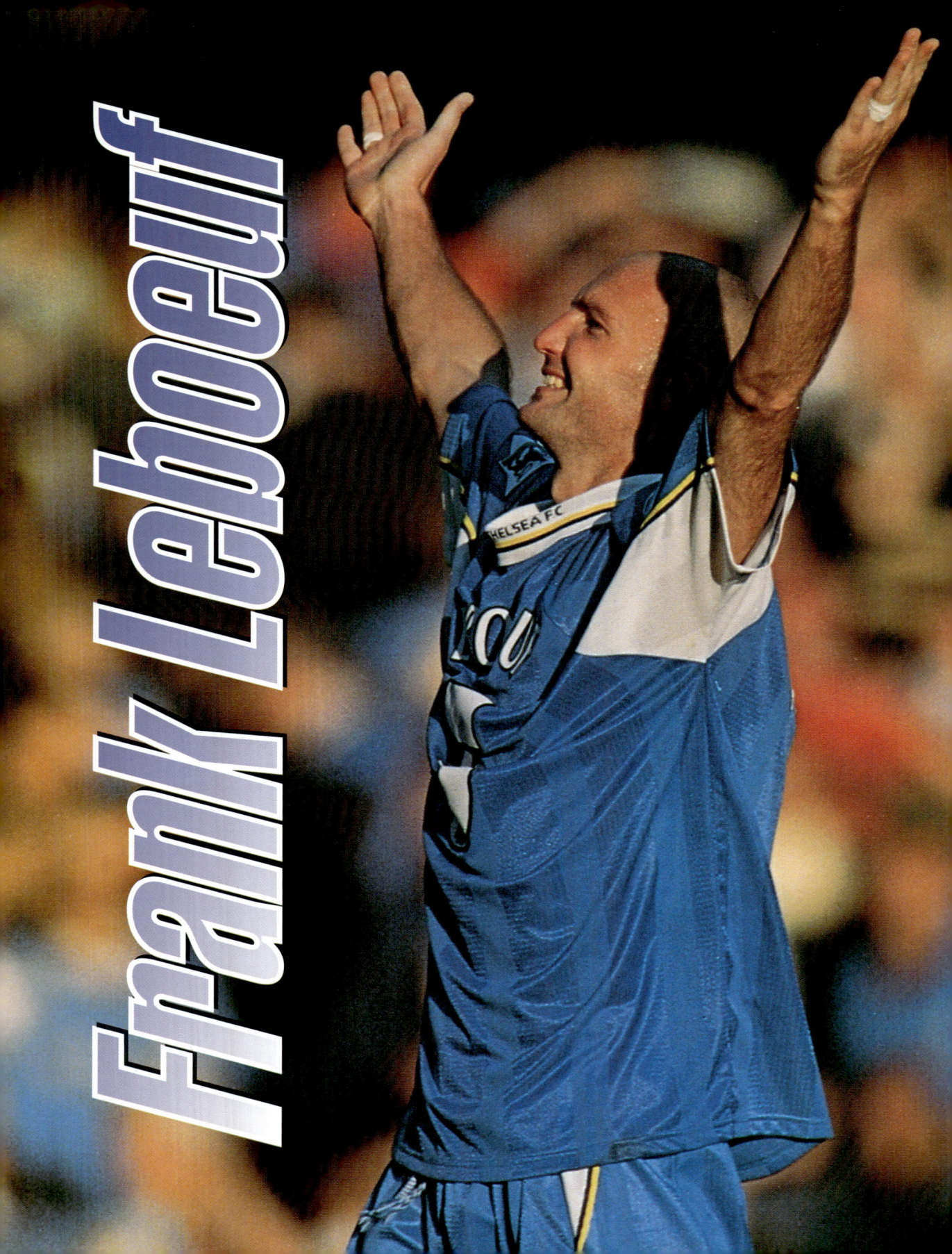

Frank Leboeuf

Best meal: 'Oysters and frogs' legs.'
Worst meal: 'Fish and chips.'
Best CD: 'Supertramp, the compilation.'
Best computer game: 'I don't play.'
Best goal: 'Mark Hughes against Crystal Palace last season from my long pass. It was fantastic how he volleyed it.'

Mostly a delight to watch, but sometimes letting a lack of concentration undo his good work, French Frank displays his huge skills best as a sweeper in a back three. Signed from Strasbourg for £2.5 million in June 1996, lanky Leboeuf got rave reviews at first for some assured displays, until he and Chelsea were duffed up by Wimbledon at Stamford Bridge. Frank recovered from that physical setback to have a fine season as the Blues finished sixth and won the FA Cup. Blessed with fine positional sense, quality tackling skills and radar-like vision, Frank can also spray the ball around both short and long and bangs away a good number of unstoppable penalties. Even stuck in the middle of a back four, where he looks less comfortable, he oozes class and self-confidence.

FRANK LEBOEUF UNPLUGGED

Describe yourself in three ways:
'I am friendly, I think that I am a little nervous and I have a big heart.'

Worst player to share a room with:
'Luca because he snores a lot.'

What would you like to achieve in your career?
'I would like to win a championship and the European Cup.'

Best thing about English football:
'Playing in a ground full of people.'

And the worst?
'When the crowd is shouting and you can't understand what they are saying – sometimes this is good if you are playing away!'

COLOUR IN FRANCO

CHELSEA SKA

For the October 1997 Cup Winners' Cup second round, Chelsea travelled to Tromsø, the most northerly professional football club in the world, located 300 miles inside the Arctic Circle on the west coast of Norway.

With the city already covered in snow, the pitch was passed fit just 45 minutes before kick-off and was in an atrocious state. The Blues failed to come to terms with the conditions and fell behind after five minutes when Nilsen crashed home from 25 yards. Worse followed when de Goey fumbled in Fermann's shot on 18. A half-time blizzard made the conditions farcical and play was stopped twice to clear snow from the lines. In a frantic finish, Vialli slithered his way through for a priceless goal after 85 minutes, Årst took advantage of confusion over a substitution to get Tromsø's third a minute later, then Vialli skated through for another important away goal on 90.

> '*It was ridiculous. I told them just lump it and see where the ball lands. You can't play, you can't dribble, just lump it there and fight. And then the class of Luca made the difference.*'
>
> *A frozen Ruud Gullit*

> '*We were a bit lucky because we had three or four chances and scored twice – they had six or seven very good chances and missed a lot of them.*'
>
> *Gianluca Vialli*

TE ON THIN ICE

... and scores in the snow

COLOUR IN ROBBIE

Ed de Goey

Signed from Feyenoord for £2.25 million last close season, Chelsea's tallest-ever player made a nervy start at Coventry that had some talking of a mistake. But the big-hearted Dutchman, who had won a Dutch Championship and four Dutch FA Cups with the Rotterdam club, showed his character and won the crowd with some match-saving displays. Most notable were the saves in the first leg of the Coca-Cola Cup semi-final at Arsenal which gave the Blues a fighting chance of making the Final, and a fine display at Real Betis when the home team threatened to overhaul Chelsea's two-goal lead. His hold on the position was only threatened by Dmitri Kharine's return from injury, but it says much for Mr Ed that he kept his form when Vialli announced his controversial policy of rotating the 'keepers.

ED DE GOEY UNPLUGGED

Best performance in Europe:

'Probably against Real Zaragoza at home two or three years ago when I was at Feyenoord. We won 1–0 and I made some good saves. It was the first leg and we did very well to beat them.'

Difference between being a goalkeeper here and in Holland

'The players can do more against the goalkeeper here than in Holland. When you go in the air they can kick you and the referee can let it go.'

Do you prefer punching to catching the ball?

'When I can help the players and catch it, I will do that. But sometimes it is better to punch it away because there are too many risks.'

PAUL HUGHES FACTFILE

Date of birth: 19 April 1976

Signed: July 1994, from Juniors

Debut: Derby County (h), 18 January 1997, as half-time substitute for Dennis Wise

Score: Chelsea won 3–1

Goal: On 84 minutes, with the Blues 2–1 up, Paul took the ball on the halfway line, played a one-two with Di Matteo to get up the line, played another with Mark Hughes to get past the last defender and slotted it past a hesitating Russell Hoult in goal. The other players celebrated by bowing down to his feet and the crowd chanted 'Hughesy!' to a new Hughes

'I was well pleased with the goal – but the most important thing was that I played well while I was out there. The goal just topped it off really. As for the celebration – nothing to do with me, but it was brilliant!'

THEY SCORED

DAVID LEE FACTFILE

Date of birth: 26 November 1969

Signed: July 1988, from Juniors

Debut: Leicester City (h), 1 October 1988, as substitute for Darren Wood

Score: Chelsea won 2–1

Goal: With Chelsea 1–0 down and struggling, David latched on to Kerry Dixon's knock-down of Kevin McAllister's cross and bundled the ball home by the post. David was also brought down for the penalty which won the game

'Bobby Campbell just said play midfield, get forward as much as you can. Someone crossed it in, Kerry headed it goalwards, the 'keeper made the save and I got in the rebound. Then I played a one-two with Kevin Wilson – I was just about to shoot, the geezer pulled me back and Robbo scored the penalty. Campbell was delighted – it was the first time I had to do loads of interviews afterwards. I enjoyed it.'

EDDIE NEWTON FACTFILE

Date of birth: 13 December 1971

Signed: May 1990, from Juniors

Debut: Everton (a), 2 May 1992, as substitute for Graeme Le Saux

Score: Chelsea lost 1–2

Goal: From a Damian Matthew free-kick the ball fell to Eddie on the edge of the area and he cracked home a right-foot volley from 20 yards to pull a goal back near the end

'I had to come on at left-back at half-time. I was playing against Beardsley and thinking "Hell!" because we only had ten men. Ken Monkou had been sent off and I had Beardsley running at me and whoever was playing right-back. I had two v one against me every time. We got a free-kick which came back out to me and I smacked it from 23 yards out. It was a great strike, straight across Southall. I ran off to celebrate and was thinking, "Did I score?" because the crowd was so quiet.'

ON THEIR DEBUTS

TORE ANDRE FLO FACTFILE

Date of birth: 15 June 1973

Signed: July 1997, from SK Brann Bergen, Norway, for £300,000

Debut: Coventry City (a), 9 August 1997, as substitute for Mark Hughes

Score: Chelsea lost 2–3

Goal: Three minutes after coming on, and with the score 1–1, Flo met Di Matteo's cross with a strong header from the far post back into the near corner

'It was a good feeling. At once I was feeling like a lot of pressure had been taken off me. It's a very big thing to score in this League and in the first game is just fantastic.'

Six Semi-Finals

Chelsea reached six semi-finals in five years from 1994 to 1998. In the previous 20 years they had reached just two. Players say it's worse to lose in a semi-final than at any other stage of a Cup competition. So near to the glory of a Final, yet so far. Well, Chelsea have won their share of semi-finals recently. Here is the story of the Cup road to nowhere – and to glory.

PEACOCK PUTS BLUE TAILS UP

1994 FA Cup Semi-Final vs Luton Town at Wembley

What an occasion! Chelsea's first FA Cup semi for 24 years, a packed Wembley with Blues fans in the majority and a simple 2–0 win courtesy of two goals from Gavin Peacock. All that and a rousing reception at the end for old hero Kerry Dixon, by now playing for Luton.

'I've been to Wembley a few times, and I can assure you the volume of support was fantastic.'
Glenn Hoddle

'The fans showed me they haven't forgotten what I gave the club.'
Kerry Dixon

Peacock puts Chelsea 1–0 up in 1994

Peacock finishes Luton with his second goal at Wembley

REAL HEARTBREAKERS

1995 European Cup Winners' Cup Semi-Final vs Real Zaragoza (Spain)

Chelsea's first European campaign since 1971 ended in a 3–4 aggregate defeat to the eventual winners of the trophy, but after a 0–3 reverse in the first leg, pride was restored at the Bridge with a 3–1 win. Magnificent atmospheres at both games showed just how vibrant European football occasions can be.

'I've said to the players I'm proud of them. They should be proud of themselves.'
Glenn Hoddle

6

Paul Furlong tussles with Gustavo Poyet, then a Zaragoza player, in the Cup Winners' Cup semi-final first leg in Spain, 1995

Ruud heads his semi-final goal at Villa Park, 1996

RUUD ALMOST HEADS TO WEMBLEY

1996 FA Cup Semi-Final vs Manchester United at Villa Park

Another year, another huge occasion, with Chelsea fans massively outsinging their rivals, and a chance to get revenge for Wembley 1994. It was not to be, but it was a pulsating game with the result in doubt until the final whistle. Beckham hit the post for United early on, then Michael Duberry chipped against the bar before the Blues took a half-time lead via the head of Ruud Gullit. The second half was heart-breaking – injuries to full-backs Steve Clarke and Terry Phelan upset the Blues, Cole and Beckham scoring United's two goals in a four-minute spell. A minute after their second, Cantona cleared off the line from John Spencer with Schmeichel beaten. Manchester 2, Chelsea 1.

6

'I can't fault the lads' effort – they put everything into it. It was a smashing game.'
Glenn Hoddle

'We want to thank everyone for their support. They were tremendous for us.'
Ruud Gullit

DONS BROUGHT DOWN
1997 FA Cup Semi-Final vs Wimbledon at Highbury

'As soon as we scored we were never going to lose. Erland and Frode were top class and Wimbledon got dispirited.'

Mark Hughes

Wimbledon have been a bogey team for Chelsea down the years, but this time there were no mistakes. Erland Johnsen and goalkeeper Frode Grodås withstood the expected Dons onslaught, and the nerves of another massive Blues following were calmed by Mark Hughes' opening goal just before half-time. Ecstasy followed with Gianfranco Zola's wonder goal after the break, then Hughes scored his fifth FA Cup goal of the season in injury time to make it 3-0 and book a Wembley date with Middlesbrough.

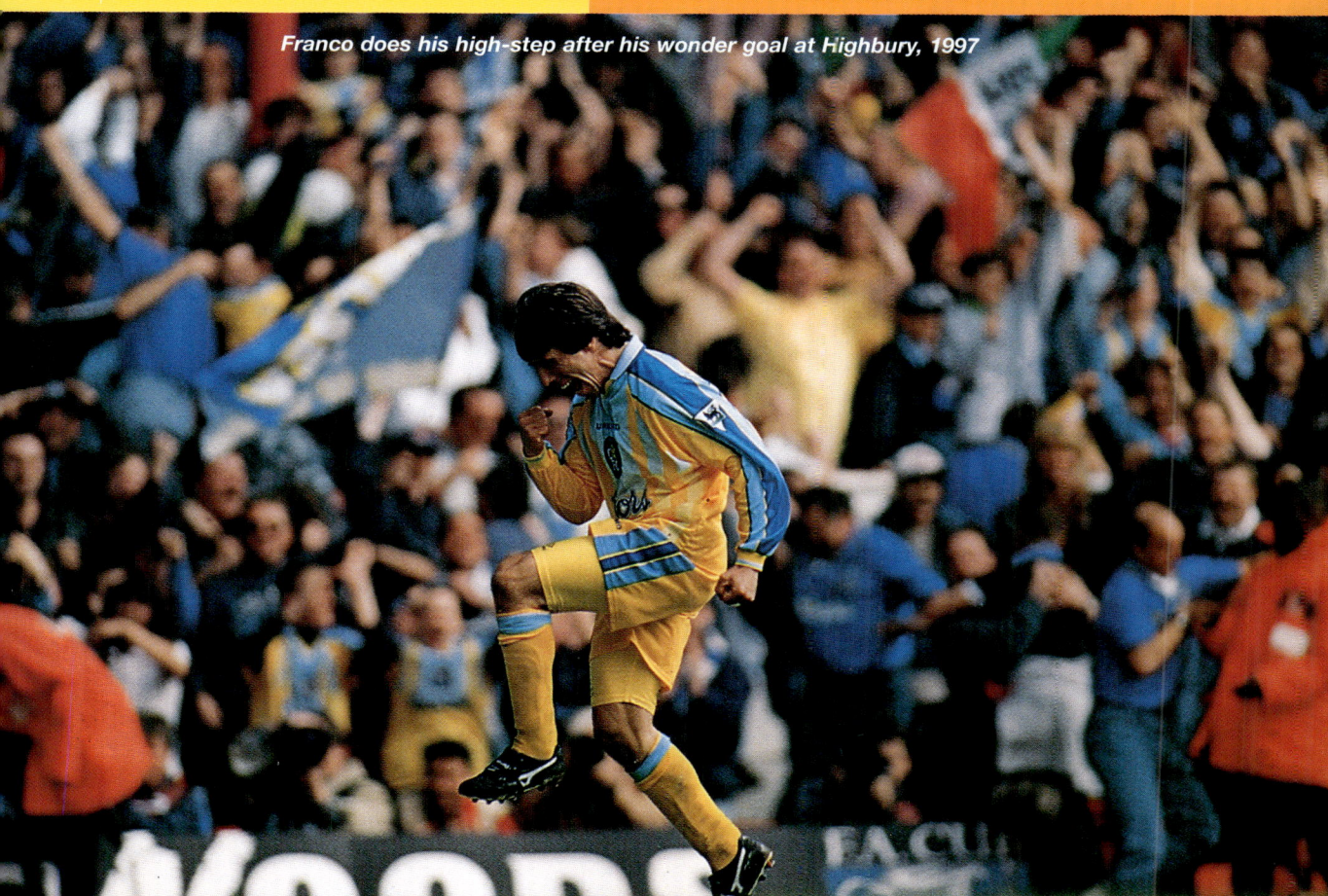

Franco does his high-step after his wonder goal at Highbury, 1997

'We got out of jail.'
Ruud Gullit after the first leg

Hughesy points the way to Wembley with the first goal in the second leg of the Coca-Cola Cup semi-final

VIALLI VICTORIOUS
1998 Coca-Cola Cup Semi-Final vs Arsenal

Two extraordinary games, and Chelsea's first semi-final win in this competition since 1972. It could all have been over in the first leg, with Arsenal two up early in the second half and forcing Ed de Goey into five magnificent saves before Mark Hughes got a priceless away goal. The second leg was Vialli's first game as player–manager, and Chelsea swept through on a tide of emotion, with the scorching second goal from Robbie Di Matteo bringing back memories of the FA Cup Final the previous year. Chelsea 3, Arsenal 1; 4-3 on aggregate.

'Before the game we had a laugh with a bit of champagne, then we did the job and we drank some champagne after the game.'
Gianluca Vialli after the second leg

HUGHES AND DE GOEY SEND CHELSEA TO STOCKHOLM

1998 European Cup Winners' Cup Semi-Final vs Vicenza

A tie that turned out to be a pulsating, thrilling affair got off to a low-key start in northern Italy. Lamberto Zauli squeezed home the only goal of the game after 15 minutes and Chelsea were grateful to Ed de Goey for a fantastic save which kept the score down.

Prospects looked bad when Pasquale Luiso made it 1-0 to Vicenza after 32 minutes at the Bridge two weeks later. Vicenza's goal came from a mistake by Duberry which found the Blues defence in no man's land and three queuing up to score. Luiso's lob-shot virtually silenced the stadium. Chelsea replied quickly. Le Saux's cross was headed out to Zola, his shot was parried by Brivio, but Poyet lashed it home. Game on.

Early in the second half, Vialli picked up a loose pass, powered down the right and hit a perfect cross for Zola which the little man nodded home. Cometh the hour, cometh the Hughes. On for just five minutes as a sub, Mark nodded on a huge de Goey kick, forced his way past Dicara and lashed a left-foot volley across Brivio and into the corner. Delirium. There was no more danger until the second minute of injury time, when Di Napoli forced his way past Clarke and sent in a low cross which Luiso looked likely to nod in at full dive – until de Goey himself dived and flipped the ball over the Italian's head. The whistle went five seconds later. Chelsea 3, Vicenza 1; 3-2 on aggregate.

'This is up there with the FA Cup Final and the Coca-Cola Cup Final. We've taken a step forward in Europe, but it's not finished yet. We know we can win the Cup. I want to say well done to the punters – they were magnificent too.'
Dennis Wise

'I'm very proud. We did something unbelievable. Sparky was magnificent. I know more than anyone how when you come off the bench it is very difficult to get into the game.'
Gianluca Vialli

All routes to Stockholm. Mark Hughes points to the Cup Winners' Cup Final after scoring the semi-final winner

Steve Clarke

Best meal: 'My mum's cooking, especially mince and tatties.'

Worst meal: 'Indian food, far too spicy for my delicate stomach.'

Best CD: 'I like all music but I'll go for The Proclaimers, a good Scottish group.'

Best computer game: 'Fifa Soccer Manager. And I've won the Premier League.'

Best goal: 'For Scotland, for the youth team in front of 95,000, played in the Aztec Stadium. It was memorable because of that. We won 1–0.'

You can ask no more of a player than that he does his best. Clarkey has done that and more for over 400 games since arriving from St Mirren in January 1987 for £422,000. In 12 seasons he's played all over the back four or five and sometimes in midfield, rarely so effectively as in the win at Derby last April when, as captain for the day, he sat in front of the defence and worked tirelessly to stamp out the threat from Baiano. It looked like his loyal service would go unrewarded in terms of silverware and then, bang, three medals in just under a year made him one of the happiest of Chelsea's Wembley celebrants. Few have deserved it more.

STEVE CLARKE UNPLUGGED

If you were given £100 to spend on clothes, what would you buy? 'I'd still shop in the same p ace – but I don't know where that is because my wife buys all my clothes. I'd rather spend £100 on a good night out.'

Coca-Cola Cup Final

Another Blue Day

'I don't believe it! I don't believe it! I don't believe it.'
Frank Sinclair, mobbed by team-mates after his goal.

'You have to believe it.'
Gianfranco Zola, lying on top of him.

'I don't believe it.'
Frank Sinclair still can't believe it.

Roberto Di Matteo gets his mobbing after goal number two

How Middlesbrough must hate Chelsea. The Wearsiders have now appeared at Wembley four times, three of them against the Blues and they haven't scored a goal in one of those three games.

At the 1998 Coca-Cola Cup Finals, however, they held out longer than 43 seconds. In fact, fielding a stronger and more united team than for the FA Cup Final the previous year, Boro looked more dangerous than Chelsea early on – but in the whole 120 minutes de Goey was not troubled by a shot on target. Goalless after 90 minutes, extra time produced two goals for Chelsea – the first a header from a delighted Frank Sinclair after Wisey pulled back a magnificent cross from the byline, the second a simple tap-in for a white-booted Di Matteo after Mustoe had slipped in attempting to clear a Zola corner. For the press, the story of the day was Paul Gascoigne's appearance as a sub for Boro – which could easily have ended in a red card after a couple of ugly challenges. For Blues fans it was the fact that Vialli went up to collect the Cup at the team's urging, having not even picked himself for a place on the bench.

Another fantastic day, and with the Cup Winners' Cup Final to come a first ever double-trophy haul was on.

Robbie and Dan eat the right stuff

FOOD GLOR
ROAST CHICKEN

If you're a professional footballer (and even if you're not) making sure you eat and drink the right things is vital – and these days most clubs take diet very seriously.

According to Terry Byrne, who ensures players get what they want and what they need before a game, the Chelsea boys generally eat foods which will give them long-term energy for the work ahead – foods known as carbohydrates. Good examples are pasta, rice and bread. At half-time they'll get a carbohydrate-rich drink and, believe it or not, jaffa cakes! 'There's no fat in jaffa cakes and they give you a quick sugar boost for energy,' says Terry. 'We also give them jelly babies for the same reason.'

Before you run off and gorge on sweets Terry points out that these should only be taken in very small doses! Another key point is that no-one drinks coffee or tea at half-time any more – the milk in tea prevents carbohydrates from being absorbed into the blood stream and so stops a player using his energy effectively.

This is what the players and staff required pre-match as the Blues were on their way to winning the 1998 Coca-Cola Cup and the European Cup Winners' Cup.

Celestine Babayaro Cheese omelette and baked beans
Laurent Charvet Roast chicken and pasta
Steve Clarke Boiled rice and fresh parmesan cheese
Neil Clement Roast chicken and baked beans
Ed de Goey Roast chicken and pasta
Roberto Di Matteo Cereals
Michael Duberry Roast chicken, mashed potato and boiled rice
Tore Andre Flo Spaghetti and bolognaise sauce
Danny Granville Pasta and spaghetti
Steven Hampshire Roast chicken and baked beans
Kevin Hitchcock Cheese and ham omelette
Mark Hughes Roast chicken breast and pasta
Paul Hughes Roast chicken and pasta
Dmitri Kharine Roast chicken and baked beans
Bernard Lambourde Cheese and ham omelette

The canteen staff: Lisa (left) and Sian

~OUS FOOD AND PASTA

Frank Leboeuf Fish, pasta and rice
Graeme Le Saux Roast chicken and spaghetti
David Lee Roast chicken and pasta
Jody Morris Roast chicken and pasta
Andy Myers Ham omelette
Eddie Newton Ham omelette
Mark Nicholls Baked beans on toast
Dan Petrescu Pasta
Gustavo Poyet Rice, pasta, parmesan cheese and fruit
Frank Sinclair Ham omelette
Gianluca Vialli White rice and roast chicken (well done)
Dennis Wise Roast chicken, white rice, pasta and baked beans
Gianfranco Zola White rice, parmesan cheese and white pasta
Graham Rix (coach) Roast chicken, baked beans and mashed potato
Gwyn Williams (assistant manager) Roast chicken and baked beans
Mike Banks (physio) Pasta and roast chicken
Terry Byrne (assistant physio) Ham omelette and baked beans
Ade Mafe (fitness and conditioning coach) Cheese omelette
Bob Orsborn (kit man) Roast chicken, mashed potato and greens

TOP TIP

'You can't exercise on an empty stomach. We want all the players to eat around three hours before a game. Afterwards you should eat something like pasta and take in small doses of sugar, such as chocolate.'

Terry Byrne, assistant physiotherapist

THE BEST DRESSING ROOM PRANKS

You're never safe from practical jokes in the Chelsea dressing room. Exploding cigars, whoopee cushions and apple pie beds have nothing on the pranks played by player on player. Remember, don't try any of these at home.

'We took all Graham Rix's clothes and put them on a skeleton, with a cigar, his Rolex watch and his trainers. It was a full-size skeleton, so no-one could tell the difference between Rixy and the skeleton.'
Kevin Hitchcock

'During pre-season we were staying at Nigel Mansell's hotel. Hitchy and Craig Burley put a dead bird in Ade Mafe's bed. Ade thought it was all that "witch doctor" stuff and went into one – he wanted a changed bed, a changed everything. I think he wanted to go home.'
Michael Duberry

'Once we were staying in Sligo in Ireland. We all broke into Kevin Wilson's room with pillow cases on our heads, pinned him down and threatened to shave his moustache off. Wisey had the razor but couldn't bring himself to do it, so we just chucked buckets of cold water on him.'
Kevin Hitchcock

'Vinnie Jones and Wisey went into Kevin Wilson's room, removed everything and put it outside the lift. When he got outside the lift on his floor, the room was just there.'
Kevin Hitchcock

'Gianfranco was reading an English book. He took it to every game and read one chapter. He was hoping to finish it by the end of the season, but he left it aside one day, so I ripped the last two chapters out. When he got to the end, he just couldn't understand why it ended there. He came into the dressing room, saw the missing pages and threw the book at me. We were all laughing but I didn't say anything. Later that evening he scored his first goal for three months against Crystal Palace. When we were running back to the centre I whispered to him "I'll give you those missing pages now."'
Dennis Wise

'Unbeknown to me, David Lee and Gareth Hall broke into Andy Townsend and Peter Nicholas' room. Andy got me to go into Dave Lee and Gareth's room with him and we tipped it upside down. We made a mess. I found some golf clubs under one of the beds, but we didn't know whose they were – so Andy and me chucked them into the swimming pool. The next day, a golf day, we were standing on the tee when Peter Nicholas went to pull his golf clubs out of his bag – it was full of broomsticks. He wasn't very happy. Only when the chaps decided to have a five-a-side in the swimming pool did they discover the missing golf clubs.'
Kevin Hitchcock

Hitchy and Luca stuggle home after their faces were superglued together (do NOT try this at home!)

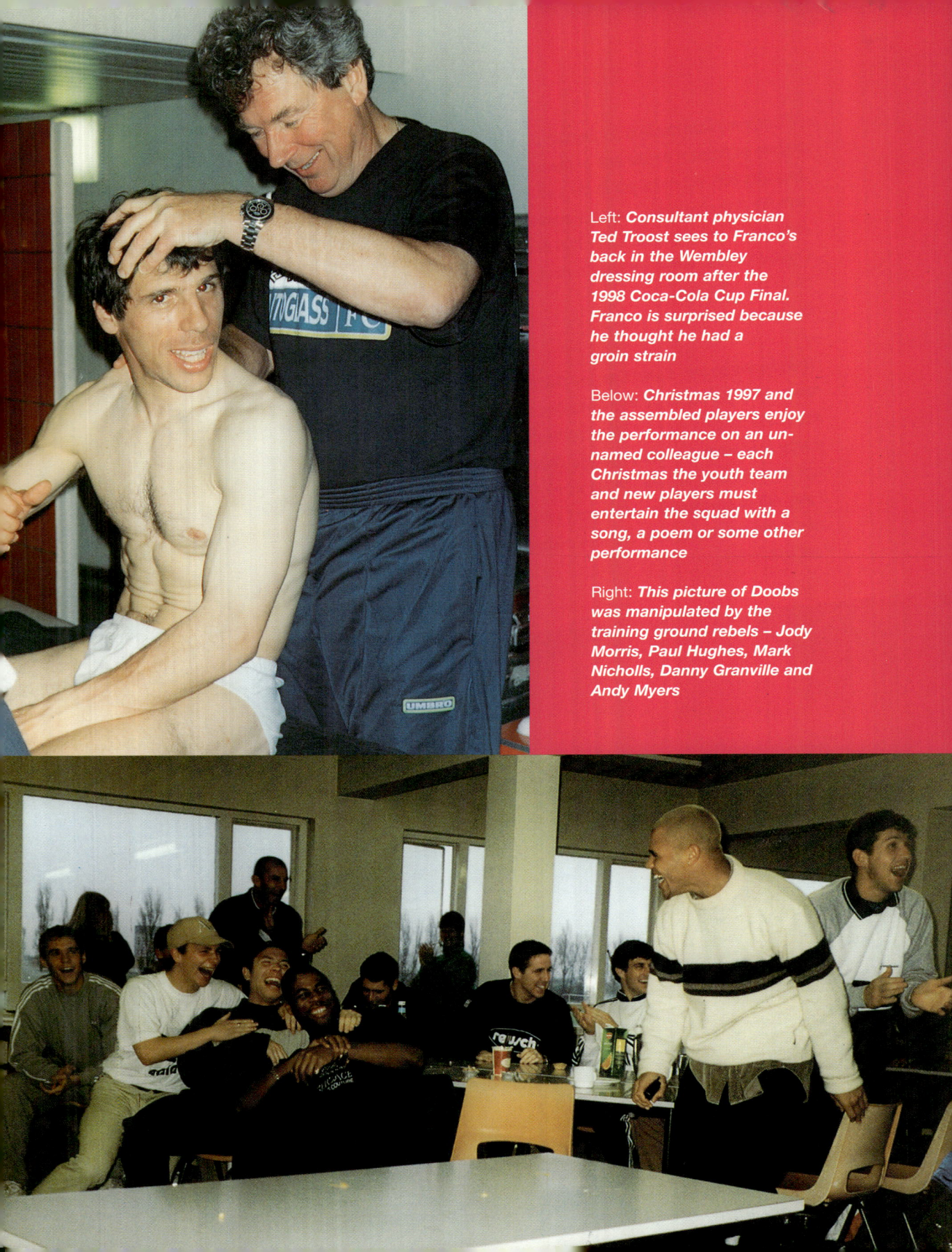

Left: *Consultant physician Ted Troost sees to Franco's back in the Wembley dressing room after the 1998 Coca-Cola Cup Final. Franco is surprised because he thought he had a groin strain*

Below: *Christmas 1997 and the assembled players enjoy the performance on an un-named colleague – each Christmas the youth team and new players must entertain the squad with a song, a poem or some other performance*

Right: *This picture of Doobs was manipulated by the training ground rebels – Jody Morris, Paul Hughes, Mark Nicholls, Danny Granville and Andy Myers*

Do I Not Like That!

Worst Team

Steve Clarke 'Bristol City reserves - away! In the first team it's got to be Arsenal because I've never played in a winning team against them away from home.'

Michael Duberry 'Manchester United. They're a very good side, never give anything away and it's never an easy game.'

Tore Andre Flo 'Arsenal or Manchester United. It's hard to say which. They have these big strong guys as defenders. They don't let you move.'

Mark Hughes 'Arsenal. They are so strong physically. Everybody hates Arsenal!'

Graeme Le Saux 'There's none that jumps to mind. You have to go into every game positively.'

Jody Morris 'Liverpool, because their midfield is very strong and they've got good movement and pass the ball well. It's hard to get over them.'

Andy Myers 'Manchester United. As well as we play them they always manage to get a draw and it winds me up. Take this season at their place, we should have won and they sneaked a draw.'

Mark Nicholls 'Brighton reserves. They just cut lumps out of you and launch it.'

Dan Petrescu 'Leeds. I don't like the style they play. I just hope we can win against them always.'

Gianfranco Zola 'I don't like to play against teams that have beaten me in the past. It's a really good thing to play against Manchester United or Arsenal or Liverpool because it's a big game. But life is hard in these games.'

Worst Player

Michael Duberry 'Alan Shearer. He's one hell of a player and the hardest opponent you'll come across in the Premier League. As a defender you don't want to play against him.'

Tore Andre Flo 'Ronny Johnsen. I think he's one of the best defenders in England. He's from Norway too. He is not easy to pass.'

Graeme Le Saux 'Andrei Kanchelskis, formerly of Manchester United and Everton. Thankfully he's now at Fiorentina. He was a fairly quick, skilful player and always managed to give you a hard time.'

Jody Morris 'Nicky Butt. He's brilliant. He's hard and he can play as well.'

Andy Myers 'Roy Keane. He's a good player but his temperament lets him down. He always wants to fight the world.'

Mark Nicholls 'Matt Elliott of Leicester. He's strong in the air, quick, good on the floor and powerful.'

Waddle, surely the worst haircut ever

Dan Petrescu 'David Batty. I just don't like him as a player. He's difficult to play against. Very hard.'

Gianfranco Zola 'No names but I don't like those players who only play to stop you or to hurt you.'

WORST GROUND

Steve Clarke 'Bristol Rovers reserves! For the first team it's just got to be Cowdenbeath. Why? If you ever get a chance to go there you will know why it's the worst.'

Michael Duberry 'Selhurst Park. Not one for atmosphere.'

Graeme Le Saux 'Barnsley. It's quite dated inside but I have to say that their supporters were some of the best I've heard this season. Even at 6–0 down they were still singing.'

Jody Morris 'Plough Lane in the reserves because it's always freezing in the dressing rooms.'

Andy Myers 'Selhurst Park. When you play Wimbledon there's hardly any atmosphere. Most of the supporters are ours.'

Mark Nicholls 'Brighton. It's on a slope and it was horrible. But they don't play there any more now.'

Dan Petrescu 'Leeds. The ground is not the best. I don't feel very good when I play against them.'

WORST HAIRCUT

Steve Clarke 'It's got to be Chris Waddle when it was spiky on top and long down the back. Sorry, Chris, it wasn't doing it for me!'

Michael Duberry 'Don Goodman of Wolves. I saw him when he scored the winner to knock Leeds out of the FA Cup and that hair...! It wasn't an afro, it wasn't dreads, it was just in-between everything.'

Mark Hughes 'I can't say mine because my wife cuts it! Frank Leboeuf because he's got a zipper at the back of his head. Or at least that's what it looks like but it's actually a big scar.'

Graeme Le Saux 'Emerson at Middlesbrough last season. He'd got a 1982 haircut and it was 1997. Saturday Night Fever or what!'

Jody Morris 'John King in the youth team when he had his blond highlights. It was a disgrace and the boys had to persuade him to get it cut because he was letting Chelsea down.'

Gianfranco Zola 'In football Roberto Di Matteo's shaved head! But one of the worst I have seen in sport is not a footballer but a volleyball player called Lucchetta. Short haircut on top at the front and then it becomes longer on top further back and it's all stuck in position with gel. It's horrible.'

THE BIG THREE

'I really believe this club is ready to take off. Success and trophies can only be around the corner. There has been a massive progression throughout the club.'

GLENN HODDLE: 1993-1996

Only five managers have taken the Blues to the FA Cup Final. Glenn Hoddle was the fourth, taking Chelsea in 1994 to their first final in 24 years. The 0-4 defeat by Manchester United was disappointing, as were final League positions of 14th, 11th and 11th in each of his three seasons in charge – but a new era began with Glenn. He brought in a new style of football, leading by example as player–manager in his first two years; he brought in Continental training techniques, including better meals for the players and a masseur; he brought European football for the first time since 1971 and almost won the Cup Winners' Cup; and, most importantly of all, he brought in Ruud Gullit. But when the chance came to manage England he couldn't refuse.

GLENN HODDLE FACTFILE

Born: Hayes, Middlesex, 27 October 1957

Previous clubs: Tottenham Hotspur, AS Monaco, Swindon Town

Signed: July 1993, from Swindon for £75,000 plus £2,000 for each of his first 50 games

Chelsea debut: Blackburn (h), 14 August 1993 – Chelsea lost 1–2

Appearances for Chelsea: 39 (including 17 as sub), 1 goal

Club honours: FA Cup winner's medals 1981 and 1982, FA Cup runners-up medal 1987, UEFA Cup winner's medal 1984 (Tottenham); French League Championship medal 1988 (Monaco); First Division play-off winner 1993 as player–manager (Swindon)

International honours: 53 England caps, 8 goals; 2 England B caps, 1 goal; England Youth; played in 1980 and 1988 European Championship finals, and in 1982 and 1986 World Cup finals

RUUD GULLIT: 1996–1998

An emotional final game of the season on 5 May 1996 – when the crowd endlessly chanted 'Ruudi, Ruudi' – saw Gullit established as the fans' favourite to take over from Hoddle. Though he'd never managed before, the Chelsea board took the risk and the Blues never looked back. That first Ruud season, too, ended in emotional scenes – this time at Wembley as the Blues won the FA Cup for the first time in 27 years.

Apart from silverware, he also brought style back to Chelsea, beginning a foreign revolution which saw Italian internationals Gianluca Vialli, Robbie Di Matteo and Gianfranco Zola arrive at the Bridge, along with France's Frank Leboeuf, to be followed in 1997 by Uruguay's Gustavo Poyet, Nigeria's Celestine Babayaro and Dutch international 'keeper Ed de Goey. And, for the first time since 1956, Chelsea signed a current England international in left-back Graeme Le Saux. At last Chelsea was the place to be, whether player or supporter.

> *'You need challenges, and this one was another. I took it and succeeded thanks to the players. I feel I've grown up as a person.'*
> *Ruud Gullit after the 1997 FA Cup Final*

RUDD GULLIT FACTFILE

Born: Amsterdam, Holland, 1 September 1962

Previous clubs: Haarlem, Feyenoord, PSV Eindhoven, AC Milan (two spells), Sampdoria (two spells)

Signed: June 1995 on a free transfer

Chelsea debut: Everton (h), 19 August 1995 – 0–0 draw

Appearances for Chelsea: 64 (including 14 as sub), 7 goals

Club honours: Dutch League Championship medal, Dutch FA Cup winner's medal 1984 (Feyenoord); Dutch League Championship medals 1986 and 1987, Dutch Footballer of the Year 1986 and 1987 (PSV Eindhoven); European Cup winner's medals 1989 and 1990, World Club Championship and European Super Cup winner's medals 1990, Italian league Championship medals 1988, 1992 and 1993 (AC Milan); Italian Cup winner's medal 1994 (Sampdoria)

International honours: 65 Holland caps, 16 goals; 4 Holland under-21 caps, 1 goal; Holland Youth; captained Holland to the 1988 European Championships in Germany, scoring one of the two goals in the final which beat the Soviet Union, and was voted second best player of the tournament; World and European Footballer of the Year 1987; also played in 1990 World Cup finals and 1992 European Championship finals

GIANLUCA VIALLI

A superstar in his own country who wants to become a Chelsea legend, Gianluca Vialli became the Blues' third consecutive player–manager in extraordinary circumstances when Gullit was sacked with Chelsea second in the League and on the verge of a Wembley final. The Blues got to Wembley by beating Arsenal on an emotional night at the Bridge in Luca's first game in charge, and then went on to take back to Stamford Bridge the club's second piece of silverware in two years when they beat Middlesbrough 2–0 at Wembley. More astonishingly still, the Blues went on to win the Cup Winners' Cup in Stockholm.

'I will try to do my best. Of course I'll make mistakes, but I'll be like a sponge – absorbing things from everyone, learning, then making decisions. And I will make decisions because it's my botty on the line.'

GIANLUCA VIALLI FACTFILE

Born: Cremona, Italy, 9 July 1964
Previous clubs: Cremonese, Sampdoria, Juventus
Signed: May 1996 on a free transfer
Chelsea debut: Southampton (a), 18 August 1996 – 0-0 draw
Appearances for Chelsea: 68 (including 18 as sub), 30 goals
Club Honours: Italian league Championship medal 1991, Italian Cup winner's medals 1985, 1988 and 1989, European Cup Winners' Cup winner's medal 1990 (Sampdoria); Italian League Championship medal, Italian Cup winner's medal 1995, UEFA Cup winner's medal 1993, European Cup winner's medal as captain 1996 (Juventus); FA Cup winner's medal 1997, European Cup Winners' Cup winner's medal 1998 (Chelsea)
International honours: 59 Italian caps, 16 goals; 20 Italian under-21 caps, 11 goals; Italian Youth. Played in 1986 and 1990 World Cup finals and 1988 European Championship finals

Gianluca Vialli

It's still hard to believe he's here, the Italian superman with a silverware collection bigger than most clubs are blessed with, but a modest charm which ensures the Chelsea faithful love him as one of their own. After a glorious career in Italy with Cremonese, Sampdoria and Juventus, he arrived at Stamford Bridge declaring: 'I want to be a Chelsea legend.' He's had his problems with fitness and with selection, but scored 10 goals in his first 16 starts against Premiership sides, banged them away regularly in his second season and lifted a Wembley trophy in only his ninth game in charge. Surely a legend in his own lifetime, and now he's a European trophy-winning manager too.

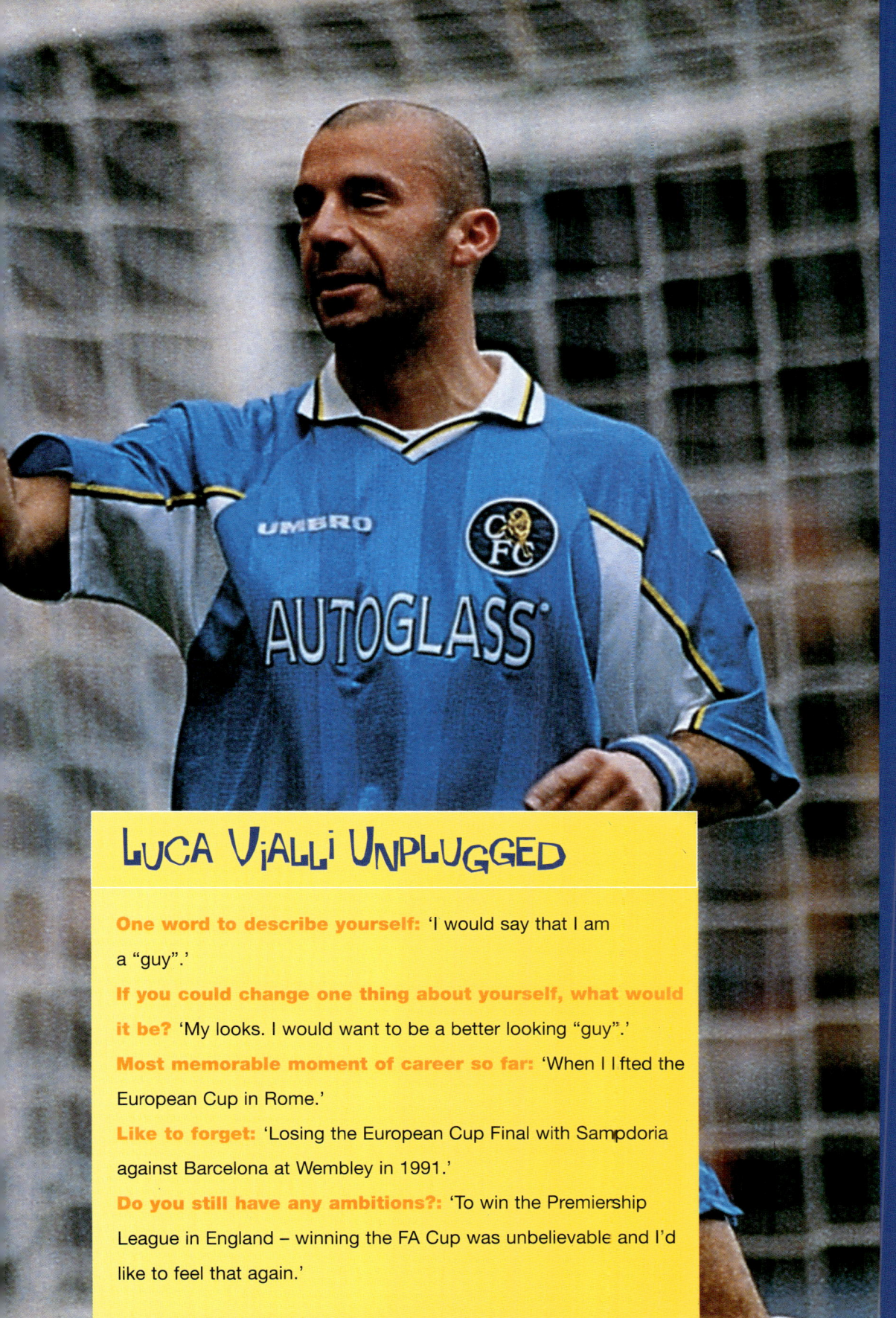

LUCA VIALLI UNPLUGGED

One word to describe yourself: 'I would say that I am a "guy".'

If you could change one thing about yourself, what would it be? 'My looks. I would want to be a better looking "guy".'

Most memorable moment of career so far: 'When I lifted the European Cup in Rome.'

Like to forget: 'Losing the European Cup Final with Sampdoria against Barcelona at Wembley in 1991.'

Do you still have any ambitions?: 'To win the Premiership League in England – winning the FA Cup was unbelievable and I'd like to feel that again.'

CUP WINNERS' CUP GLORY IN SWEDEN

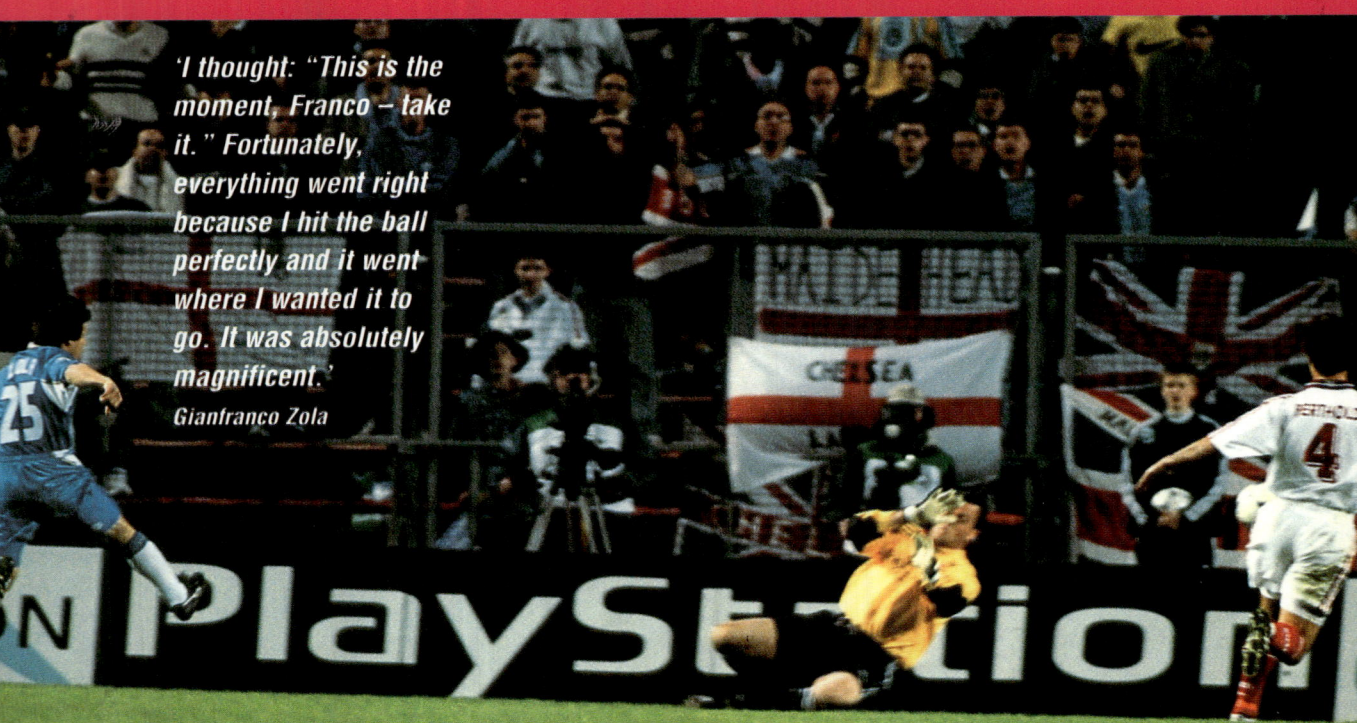

'I thought: "This is the moment, Franco – take it." Fortunately, everything went right because I hit the ball perfectly and it went where I wanted it to go. It was absolutely magnificent.'
Gianfranco Zola

This was the huge European final we'd been waiting 27 years for. On 13 May 1998 Swedish capital Stockholm was invaded – peacefully – by somewhere approaching 20,000 Blues fans. The Råsunda stadium, scene 40 years earlier of Pelé's first World Cup Final, was a sea of blue and white, with just two small areas favouring the red and white of Germany's Stuttgart.

Despite the support it was not plain sailing. After Robbie Di Matteo put a good 6th minute chance past the post, Stuttgart gave as good as they got in the first half. First a mistake by Steve Clarke set captain Fredi Bobic free, but he wastefully screwed the ball wide, then a run by the impressive Bulgarian Krassimir Balakov ended with a smart save to his right by Ed de Goey.

However, the tide turned Chelsea's way just before half-time, with Wohlfahrt blocking a Gustavo Poyet shot and Tore Andre Flo missing narrowly with a header.

The second half was all Chelsea. Wise volleyed wide on 53 minutes and the impressive Granville – deputising for the unluckily injured Le Saux – had a skidder saved after 58. But a goal would not come – until Zola strode on in place of Flo in the 71st minute.

In a dreamlike 17 seconds, the little Sardinian wrote a glorious new chapter in Chelsea history. His first touch saw him tackled by central defender Murat Yakin, but the ball went straight to Wise, whose first-time ball into the space left by the Stuttgart defender was perfect – without another touch, Zola slammed the ball home with the outside of his right foot. Despite the harsh dismissal of Dan Petrescu for a foul there were few scares until the final whistle.

After Wisey lifted the Cup Winners' Cup, the celebrations recalled those after the FA Cup Final almost one year before. Chelsea's first ever trophy double had been confirmed.

COCA-COLA CUP AND EUROPEAN CUP WINNERS' CUP